Sin

Sin

THE EARLY HISTORY
OF AN IDEA

Paula Fredriksen

PRINCETON UNIVERSITY PRESS

PRINCETON AND OXFORD

Copyright © 2012 by Princeton University Press
Published by Princeton University Press, 41 William Street, Princeton, New Jersey 08540
In the United Kingdom: Princeton University Press, 6 Oxford Street, Woodstock,
    Oxfordshire OX20 1TW

press.princeton.edu

Library of Congress Cataloging-in-Publication Data

Fredriksen, Paula, 1951–
  Sin : the early history of an idea / Paula Fredriksen.
    pages   cm
  Includes bibliographical references and index.
  ISBN 978-0-691-12890-0 (hardback)
  1. Sin—Christianity—History of doctrines—Early church, ca. 30-600.   I. Title.
  BT715.F74 2012
  241′.309015—dc23   2011053128

British Library Cataloging-in-Publication Data is available

This book has been composed in Bodoni

Printed on acid-free paper. ∞

Printed in the United States of America

10 9 8 7 6 5 4 3 2 1

For my sister, Lisa
1957–2010

Contents

Sin

PROLOGUE

Jesus of Nazareth announced the good news that God was about to redeem the world. Some 350 years later, the church taught that the far greater part of humanity was eternally condemned. The earliest community began by preserving the memory and the message of Jesus; within decades of his death, some Christians asserted that Jesus had never had a fleshly human body at all. The church that claimed the Jewish scriptures as its own also insisted that the god who had said "Be fruitful and multiply" now actually meant "Be sexually continent." Some four centuries after Paul's death, his conviction that "All Israel will be saved" (Rm 11.26) served to support the Christian belief that the Jews were damned.

What accounts for this great variety in ancient Christian teachings? The short answer is: dramatic mutations in Christian ideas about sin. As these ideas grew and changed in the turbulence of Christianity's first four centuries, so too did others: ideas about God, about the physical universe, about the soul's relation to the body, about eternity's relation to time; ideas about Christ the Redeemer—and, thus, ideas about what people are redeemed *from*.

In this book I propose to tell the story of these dramatic mutations by focusing on seven ancient figures who together represent flash points in the development of Western Christian ideas about sin. Chapter 1, "God, Blood, and the Temple," concentrates on two of these figures. The first, Jesus of Nazareth, left no writings of his own; but the gospel traditions from and about him, surviving in Greek, provide us with glimpses both of the historical figure and of the various refractions of his legacy from forty to seventy years after his death. Our second figure, Paul, never knew the historical Jesus; but he was in contact with several, perhaps many, of Jesus' original followers, and he became a tireless spokesman for his own understanding of the gospel message, which he took to pagan audiences. Paul wrote (more accurately, dictated) letters to these communities, of which seven survive in the New Testament. Composed mid-first century CE, these letters represent the earliest writings of the Jesus movement. Together with the gospels, Paul's letters would be continuously interpreted and reinterpreted as later Christians contested with each other over the tradition's true message and meaning.

Chapter 2, "Flesh and the Devil," brings us into the second century, a period of vital and vigorous diversity. Of all the figures whose work we know or know about—and there are many—I concentrate specifically on three: Valentinus, Marcion, and Justin. These three thinkers cluster in the first half of the century. Each represents distinctly different ways of adjusting the earlier Christian message to its new cultural parameters. But Justin, through his energetic repudiation of Valentinus and Marcion, set up a dynamic interaction among their three different theologies, one that eventually established the broad lines of later orthodox tradition. Justin's insistence that Jewish scriptures, understood spiritually, encode Christianity; that not only pagan worship but also—and no less—Jewish worship are sinful and religiously wrong; that salvation from sin is available uniquely through Christ, as understood uniquely by the "true church"; that such salvation requires the redemption of the body: all of these points of principle, which Justin articulated against his Christian competitors mid-century, will echo throughout the evolving tradition that claims for itself the status of orthodoxy.

Chapter 3, "A Rivalry of Genius," compares, finally, the work of two of the towering intellects of the ancient church, Origen of Alexandria and Augustine of Hippo. Each of these men draws deeply on orthodoxy's scriptures, Old Testament and New, and each draws no less deeply on the intellectual patrimony of late Platonism. Each stands within the parameters of orthodoxy as represented by Justin, and yet each produces ideas about sin—and, thus, about the world, humanity, and God—that could not contrast more sharply with those of the other. Of the two, Origen represents the road not taken by the church, whereas Augustine became a font of subsequent Latin Christian doctrine. In the epilogue, finally, I will bring together all of our figures to see once more how and where they differ from each other, and to offer some brief closing thoughts on the ways that the idea of sin, so important in antiquity, now seems to figure in contemporary American culture.

～～～

This essay draws upon my three Spencer Trask Lectures, which I had the privilege to give at Princeton University in October 2007. While I have substantially augmented my original presentation, I have kept my focus on the seven figures mentioned above precisely because they contrast and compare so vividly and, I think, usefully. A true historical survey of ancient ideas of sin would necessarily include many more figures, and it would be a lot longer than the present work. An investigation of gradual change—the incremental transformation of prior materials and traditions—could also, in a much longer book, wend its stately way. And a more phenomenological approach would dwell on the various ways in which ancient actors gave voice to the experience of sin, to their feelings in the face of moral failure, of regret, of the mysterious brokenness of the world. Such a study, in short, would be a very different book.

I have elected here instead to sketch a staccato history of early Christian ideas about sin by focusing on those moments that represent evolutionary jumps—points of "punctuated equilibrium," as evolutionary biologists say. I attend not to reflections on the experience of sin but instead to its very various conceptualizations; not to long-lived continuities, but to dramatic changes. Of course, the Bible itself, whether in its Jewish or its Christian forms, represents a fundamental line of continuity: all of our thinkers support their own views via appeals to its authority. But they each think about biblical tradition differently. And while Greek-speaking diaspora Jews centuries before Paul had already produced various fusions of Hellenistic and Jewish thought, I concentrate here on Paul himself, and on the ways that the apocalyptic message of the crucified and returning messiah charges and changes his view of the Hellenistic cosmos and of Stoic moral psychology. Finally, while various Christian communities could express many shades of conviction on the continuum between fervent belief in the imminent end of all things and (no less) fervent belief in history's *longue durée*, I concentrate on contrasts. *Disjunctures* are what I want to lift up here.[1]

To begin to trace the rich and complex story of early Christian ideas about sin, we need to begin where they began: within the matrix of late Second Temple Judaism. Three first-century Jews will be our guides: in the land of Israel, John the Baptist and Jesus of Nazareth; and in the western, Greek-speaking Diaspora, the apostle Paul. Our journey through this early history starts at a time when leprosy and death defiled, when fire and water made clean, and when one approached the altar of God with purifications, blood offerings, and awe. We begin with the message that the god of Israel was about to redeem his people and establish his kingdom; and that message itself, for Christianity, begins by the River Jordan.

Chapter 1
GOD, BLOOD, AND THE TEMPLE

Jesus and Paul on Sin

"The time is fulfilled, and the kingdom of God is at hand. Repent, and trust in the good news!" Thus the first words of Jesus' mission according to the Gospel of Mark (1.15). But Mark frames Jesus' proclamation by opening his story with another charismatic figure, John the "Baptizer," whom he introduces some ten verses earlier. John also called out for repentance, Mark states there. But his mission had been coupled with immersion in the Jordan "for the forgiveness of sins," and the people who streamed out to John "confessed" their sins as he submerged them (1.4–5). Jesus' immersion by John—a tradition securely attested in the gospel material—implies that he approved of and consented to John's message and that his own mission in some sense was a continuation of John's.[1]

"Baptism" for the remission of sin would go on to have a long future as a sacrament of the church. That later institution casts a giant shadow backward, obscuring what Mark tells us in the opening verses of his gospel. Jesus' unadorned statement quite simply defies any idea of a long future. In announcing the imminent arrival of God's kingdom, Jesus announced as well the impending foreclosure of normal history: "kingdom of God" is an apocalyptic concept. The Baptizer's call to penitent sinners seems likewise to have been motivated by his own apocalyptic convictions. "Repent, because the kingdom of heaven is at hand," Matthew's John teaches (3.2). And the Baptizer warns of looming final judgment by God's coming agent: "His winnowing fork is in his hand . . . he will gather his wheat into the granary, but will burn the chaff with unquenchable fire" (Mt 3.12//Lk 3.17). Finally, John's specific combination of repentance *plus* immersion conjures other religious convictions lost to the later church but vitally significant to early first-century Jews: the importance of purity rituals such as immersion in the process of repentance, which in turn entailed both the temple in Jerusalem as God's designated place of atonement and the role of offering sacrifices in making atonement.[2]

Time's end; repentance before the imminent final judgment; purity; cult; the temple: these are some of the cultural building blocks by which John the Baptizer and Jesus of Nazareth would have constructed their ideas about sin and repentance. But the gospels complicate our view of them on this issue in part because all four evangelists wrote their works sometime after—indeed, perhaps in light of—the first Jewish revolt against Rome. Recounting traditions about the life, mission, and message of Jesus, the gospels relate a narrative context that corresponds roughly to the first third of the first century, from the final years of Herod the Great (d. 4 BCE) to Pontius Pilate's term of office (26–36 CE). The gospel writers' own historical context, however—the final third of the first century—runs from the Roman destruction of Jerusalem in 70 CE to about the year 100. Between these two periods stands a traumatic rupture in Israel's traditional worship. The evangelists know what the historical John and Jesus did not know: Jerusalem's temple was no more.[3]

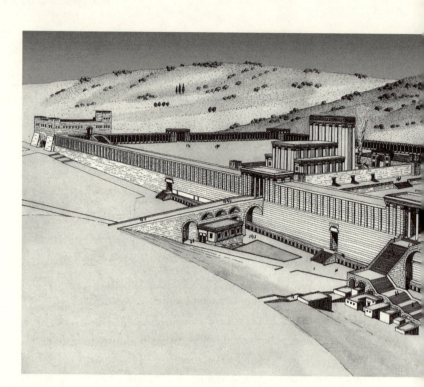

Figure 1. The Second Temple in the early Roman Empire: Jerusalem, Herod's Temple Mount, reconstruction based on archaeological and historical evidence. "Go, show yourself to the priest, and offer for your purification what Moses commanded" (Mk 1.44). The Temple in Jerusalem—to which Mark's Jesus directs the cleansed leper—was the premier site for Israel's offerings. These could be brought for many reasons: to give thanks; to mark the fulfillment of a vow; for purification, or for sin; or (especially on Yom Kippur) to make atonement. By Jesus' lifetime, thanks to the building and beautification program of Herod the Great (d. 4 BCE), the temple reached the acme of its size and splendor: the wall surrounding its largest courtyard, the Court of the Gentiles, ran almost nine-tenths of a mile. When Paul, in his letter to the community at Rome, praises God for the privileges that he has bestowed upon Israel, the apostle singles out the temple's sanctuary as the dwelling place of God's "glory" (*doxa* in Paul's Greek, resting on the Hebrew *kavod*), and as the place of his sacrificial cult (Greek *latreia*; Rom 9.4). This drawing presents a view of the Herodian Temple Mount from the southwest. Note the size of the human figures, which give a sense of its scale. Courtesy Leen Ritmeyer.

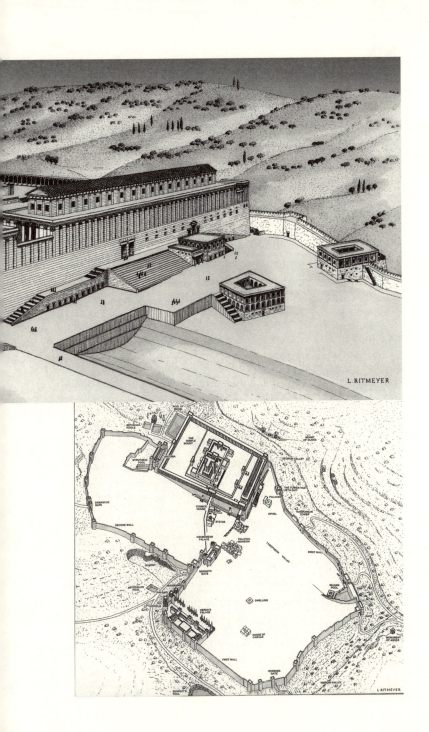

L. RITMEYER

L. RITMEYER

Both the synoptic ("seen-together") gospels—Mark, Matthew, and Luke—and the Gospel of John project knowledge of the temple's future destruction back into the lifetime of Jesus. They interpret the death of Jesus in light of the "death" of the temple, and the "death" of the temple in light of the death of Jesus. Mark, for instance, presents Jesus as hostile to the temple. In a scene traditionally described as a "cleansing," Jesus disrupts the temple's functioning (an act that leads directly to his own death; Mk 11.15–18) and predicts its destruction: "As he came out of the Temple, . . . Jesus said, 'There will not be left here one stone upon another that will not be thrown down'" (Mk 13.1–2; Mt 24.2 and Lk 21.6 follow suit). The themes of destroying and rebuilding the temple and of the death and resurrection of Jesus appear intertwined throughout Mark's passion narrative. The Fourth Evangelist, more forthrightly, combines Jesus' disrupting the temple and predicting its coming destruction into a single prophecy that actually encodes Jesus' death and resurrection: "But [Jesus] spoke of the temple of his body. When therefore he was raised from the dead, his disciples remembered that he had said this" (Jn 2.21–22). And in an even more daring conflation of Jesus and the temple, the evangelist presents Jesus himself as a sin sacrifice: "Behold the Lamb of God, who takes away the sin of the world!" (Jn 1.29).[4]

The gospels, in brief, offer both a barrier and a bridge to reconstructing the historical Jesus. Their theological commitments and the certain historical knowledge of their authors— the knowledge that God's kingdom did not arrive in Jesus' lifetime, that the temple no longer functioned, and thus that their own generation no longer offered sacrifices—contour their portraits and affect them profoundly. Yet the gospels nevertheless remain our best source of information for Jesus' life, mission, and message. Can we compensate, then, for the ways that the evangelists "updated" their various portraits to the period post-70 CE? Can we somehow historically recontextualize their traditions in order to interpret them within the pre-Christian period of Jesus' own lifetime? And if we do so, can we come to a clearer understanding of Jesus' own convictions about sin?

Here the letters of Paul can help. At first blush this may not seem obvious. After all, Paul, like the evangelists, stands at several removes from the historical Jesus of Nazareth. Jesus would have taught in Aramaic, a linguistic cousin of Hebrew; Paul, like the evangelists, thought and taught in Greek, relying on a Greek translation of the Hebrew scriptures, the Septuagint, to do so. The evangelists had no direct knowledge of Jesus, nor did Paul, as he forthrightly states (see 1 Cor 15.3). Finally, for Paul as for the evangelists, a significant shift had occurred between Jesus' audience and their own. Jesus had taught within the overwhelmingly Jewish context of the Galilee and Judea, and most specifically in Jerusalem. His audience was largely fellow Aramaic-speaking Jews. Paul, by contrast, taught within the cities of the western Greek-speaking Diaspora, the most likely setting of the evangelists, too; and his audience was predominantly (if not exclusively) gentile. While the narrative setting of the gospels precludes their depicting Jesus as engaged in a mission to gentiles, they variously present him as anticipating such a mission; and gentiles most likely numbered among the gospel communities, too. Finally, the conviction that Jesus had been raised from the dead charges everything that Paul taught. In all these ways and for all these reasons, Paul, like the evangelists, is also a "Christian" and not a "pre-Christian" writer.[5]

Yet Paul lived a full generation before the earliest gospel writer, Mark. His letters cluster at mid-first century, a fact that unites him to the historical Jesus and to the original disciples despite all the differences standing between them. Put otherwise, like Jesus of Nazareth and the original disciples, and unlike the evangelists, Paul had no knowledge of the temple's destruction. In his references to the temple, then, we may be able to catch glimpses of the ways that other early followers of Jesus—and thus, perhaps, even Jesus himself—might have thought and taught about it. Indeed, as we will shortly see, the temple and its cult remained for Paul two of the abiding privileges that God had conferred upon his people (Rm 9.4–5).[6]

Paul's letters further preserve another significant datum connecting Jesus' original disciples, and thus Jesus himself, in a positive way to the temple. According to Paul's letter to the Galatians, the early movement gave up its Galilean roots and instead, after the crucifixion, settled permanently in Jerusalem (e.g., Gal 1.18, 2.1). Why? Luke/Acts states what Paul's report implies: Jesus' disciples continued to worship in the temple (Lk 24.53; Acts 2.46). Jesus' supposed hostility toward the temple, developed in the later gospels, accordingly seems generated less from a genuine memory preserved about Jesus and more from the evangelists' own need to explain why God had allowed his temple to be destroyed. (Answer: Jesus himself had condemned the temple. Or, the temple authorities, in condemning Jesus, in turn caused God to condemn the temple. Or, Jerusalem, by not acknowledging Jesus, had sealed its own doom.) But if the historical Jesus had indeed repudiated the temple and its cult, why would his disciples still be worshiping there in the decades after his death? In light of their activity, it seems more likely that no such repudiation had ever occurred. Other traditions preserved within the gospels that suggest Jesus' piety toward the temple—such as his directive to a cleansed leper to perform there the offerings mandated by Leviticus (Mk 1.40–44 and parr.), or his expectation that his followers would make offerings at its altar (Mt 5.24), or his belief that God dwelled in the temple (Mt 23.21)—accordingly seem more secure.

Yet more than the temple itself held Jesus' disciples in Jerusalem. If we set their proclamation—that Jesus was raised from the dead and was about to return—against the huge backdrop of biblically shaped apocalyptic traditions, we see as well that they expected Jerusalem—renewed, enlarged, made beautiful—to stand at the center of God's new kingdom. Already in the classical prophets, Jerusalem had figured prominently as the place where, at the end of days, all humanity would come to worship Israel's god.

> In the days to come, the mountain of the Lord's house
> Will be established as the highest of the mountains,
> And shall be raised above the hills.
> All the nations shall stream to it.
> Many peoples shall come and say,
> "Come, let us go up to the mountain of the Lord,
> to the house of the god of Jacob; that he may teach us his ways,
> and we might walk in his paths." (Is 2.2–3)

As apocalyptic traditions developed in the late Second Temple period (c. 200 BCE—70 CE), we see the enlargement of these prophetic ideas of restoration and redemption. A battle between the forces of good and evil; the persecution of the righteous, and their ultimate vindication; the ingathering of all Israel; the nations' repudiation of their idols, and their turning to the god of Israel; the resurrection of the dead and the final judgment; the establishment of universal peace: all of these themes sound in various combinations and in various ways in Jewish apocalyptic traditions, including those later preserved in the Christian New Testament. In the period shortly after Jesus'

Jesus' own apocalyptic commitments set the time frame of his mission to call Israel to repentance; but what was its content? From what to what did he summon his hearers? We can best reconstruct Jesus' ideas on sin by turning to a core tradition of the covenant, the Ten Commandments. By Jesus' time, Jews referred to these as "the Two Tables of the Law." The first five commandments governed relationship with God; the second five, relations between people. When Josephus, the Jewish historian contemporary with the evangelists, characterizes the mission of John the Baptizer, he communicates his message by employing this pious shorthand. "John exhorted the Jews to lead righteous lives," writes Josephus, "to practice *justice* [Greek: *dikaiosune*] *toward their fellows* and *piety* [Greek: *eusebeia*] *toward God*, and in so doing to join in immersion. . . . The immersion was for the purification of the flesh once the soul had previously been cleansed through right conduct" (*Antiquities of the Jews* 18.116–19).[8]

Thus:

First Table: Piety toward God	Second Table: Justice toward Others
1. Worship no other gods	6. No murder
2. No graven images (idols)	7. No adultery
3. No abuse of God's name	8. No theft
4. Keep the Sabbath	9. No lying
5. Honor parents	10. No coveting

According to Josephus, then, the Baptizer's call to repentance—*tshuvah*, in the Hebrew of later rabbinic idiom: "turn"—thus meant, precisely, *returning* to God's commandments as revealed in the Torah. How radically new was this message? In the Jewish context presupposed by both Josephus and by the evangelists, it wasn't. And the Baptizer's emphasis on attending to the inner dimension of repentance ("cleansing the soul through right conduct" in Josephus' phrasing) before the external protocols of atonement ("purification of the flesh" through immersion) is a stock theme in Jewish penitential tradition of all periods. However, John coupled his call to recommit to the Torah both to bodily purification and to apocalyptic warnings. Those who failed to heed his warning to repent, says the John of Matthew and Luke, will "burn with unquenchable fire": "Even now the ax is laid to the root of the trees. Every tree therefore that does not bear good fruit"—that is, the fruit of repentance in Matthew 3.8—"is cut down and thrown into the [apocalyptic] fire" (Mt 3.10).[9]

John's message apparently had a major impact on Jesus. In all gospel traditions, Jesus begins his own public mission only after his immersion by John. And Jesus too, say the synoptic gospels, oriented his moral teaching by appeal to the Two Tables of the Law. Asked what were the greatest of the commandments, Jesus responds by quoting from the Torah, citing Deuteronomy 6.4 (the first line of the Jewish prayer the Sh'ma) and Leviticus 19.18. "Hear O Israel, the Lord our God, the Lord is one. And you shall love the Lord your God with all your heart, and with all your soul, and with all your might"—*eusebeia*, piety toward God (Dt 6.4); and "You shall love your neighbor as yourself"—*dikaiosune*, justice toward others (Lv 19.18; Mk 12.29–31 and parallels). In Mark's gospel, Jesus answers a sinos, Jesus wore ritual fringes—*tsitsiot* in Hebrew, *kraspeda* in Greek—whose function was to remind the wearer of God's commandments (Mk 6.56; cf. Nm 15.37–40, lines also incorporated into the Sh'ma). We can infer from all this that Jesus defined living rightly as living according to the Torah, as summed up in and by the Ten Commandments; that he defined sin as breaking God's commandments; and that he defined "repentance" as (re)turning to this covenant.

But according to teachings that appear in the Sermon on the Mount, Jesus may have been even stricter about keeping the law than the law itself required. The law said, "Do not kill"; Matthew's Jesus teaches that anyone who is even angry will be subject to judgment, "and whoever says, 'You fool!' shall be liable to the hell of fire" (Mt 5.21–22). The law said, "No adultery"; Jesus warns against even feeling lust: better to pluck out one's eye or cut off one's hand than to sin in this way and be thrown entirely into hell (5.27–30). The law, in condemning false swearing, permits swearing in principle; Jesus absolutely forbids it (5.31–37). Murder, adultery, and lying, all forbidden by the law, were sins. Whoever avoided even anger, as Matthew's Jesus teaches, or lust "in the heart" or swearing, would never contravene the law and so would not sin.[10]

Jesus' message and his modus operandi seem both like and unlike John's. Both men prophetically called out to fellow Jews to repent. But John evidently had people come to him by the Jordan, whereas Jesus sought people out, taking his message on the road, finding hearers in villages, synagogues, and market-

places, and even in the temple in Jerusale~~m~~, accor~~d-~~
ing to the synoptics, many times accor~~ding to~~
John). And while the Baptizer seems to ~~have been~~
ascetic and concerned with purity, Jesus, ~~by contrast~~
have been drawn neither to nonbiblical purifications (as convin~~c-~~
ingly reported, for example, in Mk 7.1–23) nor to John's asceticism: "John came neither eating nor drinking, and they say, 'He
has a demon'; the Son of man came eating and drinking, and
they say, 'Look! A glutton and a drunkard!'" (Mt 11.18–19//Lk
7.33–34). According (uniquely) to the Fourth Gospel, however,
and like the Baptizer, Jesus also immersed penitent sinners, as
did his disciples (Jn 3.22, 25).[11]

Finally, and again like the Baptizer, Jesus seems to have
linked his apocalyptic message to threats of divine punishment.
In material from the "Q" source—traditions common to Matthew and Luke that are not in Mark—Jesus pronounces dire
warnings against villages that rebuff him: when the kingdom
comes, he says, "it will be more tolerable on that day for Sodom
than for that town" (Mt 10.15//Lk 10.12). He calls woes down
upon Chorazin, Bethsaida, and Capernaum, Galilean villages
that did not heed his call to repentance: "If the mighty works
done in you had been done in Tyre and Sidon"—that is, in gentile cities—"they would have repented long ago, sitting in sack-
cloth and ashes" (Mt 11.20//Lk 10.13–15). Men will be judged
for every careless word on the final day, Jesus warns (Mt 12.36–
37). The men of Nineveh who repented at the call of the prophet
Jonah will judge those of Jesus' generation who did not heed
him (Mt 12.41//Lk 11.32). Good and bad fish, weeds mixed in
with wheat: it will all be sorted out at the close of the age, when
the righteous will be separated from those evildoers who will
burn in the fires of judgment, weeping and gnashing their teeth
(Mt 13.24–50, a long eschatological discourse). Better to pluck

17

out an eye, to cut off hand or foot, than to be led into sin by them, and so risk being thrown entirely into hell, "where the worm does not die and the fire is not quenched" (Mk 9.42–48 and parr.). As with John the Baptizer, then, so with Jesus: both used the threat of God's burning anger toward sinners, and the harshness of his coming judgment, to spur their listeners to repentance.

But the gospels also preserve stories of Jesus' calling out to sinners by encouraging them to consider other aspects of the biblical god's character—namely, his surpassing love, mercy, leniency, and compassion: "If you, who are evil, know how to give good gifts to your children, how much more will your Father who is in heaven give things to those who ask him!" (Mt 7.11). Heaven rejoices over the repentant sinner just as a woman rejoices over finding a lost coin, or as a father over the return of a prodigal son (Lk 15.8–32). Merciful as well as just, God loves the sinner who seeks him out no less—perhaps more—than he loves the righteous. Accordingly, the sinner who harkened to Jesus' call to repentance, Jesus taught, need not fear God's wrath. (Indeed, she should fear it less than should the righteous who did not receive Jesus' message of the coming kingdom.) Prostitutes and tax collectors who did heed Jesus would enter the kingdom before those chief priests who did not (Mt 21.31). When that day dawned, many of the first would be last, and last first (Mk 10.31 and parr.). But this good news of God's forgiveness, Jesus also taught, made an added ethical demand of the penitent sinner: as God had forgiven him, so should he forgive others, "not seven times, but seventy times seven" (Mt 18.22), generously and sincerely ("from your heart," Mt 18.35). "Forgive us our sins," Jesus taught his followers to pray, "as we ourselves forgive everyone indebted to us" (Lk11.4). God's love, and his forgiveness of human sin, in short, require an ethical reciprocity among humans, who should love, and forgive, each other.

That God forgives penitent sinners would not have come as a new message to John's or Jesus' audiences: by this time, the Jews as a people had been composing and preserving scriptures and creating liturgies embodying their faith in such a god for almost a millennium. The principle underlay the religious logic of Yom Kippur ("a day of atonement. . . . a statute for ever throughout your generations in all your dwellings," Lv 23.27–31). The newness of their message, and the reason why it sounded to their contemporaries like prophecy, then, was not because of novelty in their moral instruction. Rather, it was because of their urgency—*the kingdom was at hand*—coupled to their claim to have singular authority conferred by heaven to pronounce this message, that contemporaries regarded both John and Jesus as prophets.[12]

John enacted his prophetic authority by immersing penitents personally—a practice that the synoptic Jesus viewed as divinely sanctioned ("the baptism of John came from heaven," Mk 11.30 and parr.). Jesus, on the other hand, seems to have enacted his authority and reinforced his message of the impending end-time especially through exorcisms, a form of healing. "If it is by the finger of God [Mt: "of heaven"] that I cast out demons, then the kingdom of God has come upon you" (Mt 12.28//Lk 11.20). And according to the synoptics, Jesus' strategy worked: because news of his abilities spread, "Jesus could no longer openly enter a town, but was out in the country, and people came to him from every quarter" (Mk 1.45). These "mighty works" brought in the crowds, but the goal was to preach repentance in advance of the kingdom's arrival.[13]

Repentance in Jesus' day involved more than just genuine contrition and a resolution to change one's ways on the part of the penitent sinner. It was tied as well into long traditions of purification and sacrifices, which in turn involved the temple. And offering sacrifices for sin—which God had mandated in the covenant—in turn required bodily purification. Did Jesus accept these biblical teachings?

About sin offerings as such we have no direct knowledge: nowhere in the gospels does Jesus accompany his call to repentance, or his pronouncing of forgiveness, with explicit instructions to (ex-)sinners to offer at the temple the next time they were in Jerusalem. (An offering did not have to be brought immediately, and the great majority of Jews who lived in the Diaspora could not or did not make the trip.) Many modern people have thought, and many New Testament scholars have argued, that since Jesus did not specifically say to offer at the temple he in effect repudiated the temple and its sacrifices. The so-called cleansing of the temple is often pressed into service of this view.[14]

But as we have already seen, Paul's letters suggest, and Luke/Acts states, that the disciples continued to worship in the temple. We can infer from this that Jesus never taught them to do otherwise. But what can be reconstructed positively of Jesus' views on these intertwined issues of the centrality of the temple and its function as a place to make atonement through sacrifice?

The gospels can reveal some answers, but we can detect them only if we know something of Jewish purity laws to begin with. For example, Mark presents Jesus as giving explicit instructions to a leper whom he cleanses "to show yourself to the priest and offer . . . what Moses commanded" (Mk 1.40–44; note that Jesus *cleanses* or "purifies" the leper, he does not "heal" him; the pertinent issue is impurity, not illness). This is an uncomplicated endorsement of a very elaborate sequence of ablutions and sacrifices (a bird, two male lambs, one perfect year-old ewe), detailed in Leviticus 14, by which the leper moves from pollution to purity, from isolation back into life in the community.

Jesus' adherence to biblical purity regulations, further, unobtrusively informs the evangelists' presentation of his ascent to Jerusalem for his final Passover there. All four depict Jesus' entering the city together with a crush of other pilgrims in the week before the feast, the so-called Triumphal Entry. Why? Below the surface of this story lies the legislation given in Numbers. The pilgrim is enjoined there to eat the Paschal meal in a state of purity, including and especially purity from corpse pollution (Nm 9.6). "Those who touch the dead body of any human being shall be unclean for seven days. They shall purify themselves with the water on the third day and on the seventh day, and so be clean" (Nm 19.11–12). The "water" in question was mixed with the ashes of an entirely immolated red heifer (Nm 19.9). In the days of the Second Temple, pilgrims to Jerusalem for Passover would undergo this ritual, which was punctuated with sprinklings on the third and the seventh day. This ritual cleansing would have to be completed by 14 Nisan, when the holiday began. If Jesus indeed entered the city with the other pilgrims, and if he taught to the crowds at the temple in the week before the feast, as the gospels portray, then he was there, as were the others, for this rite of purification. Further, the Passover meal celebrated in the synoptic gospels by Jesus and his disciples also presupposes that all had been purified in order to celebrate the feast. And finally, one of their number would have had to have gone to the temple mount earlier in the day to offer the *corban Pesach*, the lamb for the Passover meal.[15]

It was at this meal, according to the synoptics, that Jesus presented wine that he had blessed as "my blood of the covenant, which is poured out for many for the forgiveness of sins" (Mk 14.24). This same tradition is refracted by Paul in 1 Corinthians 11.23–25; the bread is Jesus' body, the cup a new covenant in Jesus' blood: "As often as you eat this bread and drink the cup, you proclaim the Lord's death *until he comes*"—until he returns, that is, in order to establish God's kingdom (1 Cor 11.26; see also 1 Cor 15, passim). If something like this saying does indeed go back to the historical Jesus, then we have another oblique answer to the question, "what connections did Jesus see among sin, forgiveness, sacrifice, and the coming kingdom?" Answer: So vital a connection that he summed up his own work in exactly those terms. Had Jesus not esteemed the temple, its biblically based protocols of sacrifice, and its function as a place of atonement offerings for the forgiveness of sin, he would not have used them as the ultimate touchstone of his own mission.

~~~

With the letters of Paul we enter a different world. For one thing, it is a much larger world, both geographically and demographically. Jesus and his original disciples had kept close to territorial Israel, and had directed their mission primarily to other Jews. (Matthew's Jesus goes so far as to instruct his disciples, "Go nowhere among the gentiles, and enter no town of the Samaritans, but go rather to the lost sheep of the house of Israel"; Mt 10.5–6). By contrast, Paul ranged along the great east-west highway that tied the Greco-Roman cities of Asia Minor and Greece to Rome. And he directed his mission not to Jews but to pagans.

If Paul's world is larger than Jesus' in the positive sense of wider territory and more people, it is also larger in a negative sense: Paul's spiritual opposition is much bigger, much more powerful, and much more deeply entrenched than is that of Jesus. In the gospels, Jesus combats "demons" and "unclean spirits," low local powers that cause mental and physical illness. *The* devil, Satan, relative to these other forces plays only a cameo role (see, for example, Mk 1.13 and parr., Lk 22.3). Paul and his gentile communities combat these lesser powers, too: like Jesus' disciples (and, confusingly, even like the Christian "evildoers" whom Matthew's Jesus repudiates; Mt 7.21–23)—he and they also heal, prophesy, do works of power, and discern between spirits (identifying which are good and which bad, 1 Cor 12.6–10; for the disciples, Mt 10.7–8).

Yet Paul also battles a full panoply pagan deities, whose powers stretch from earth and below the earth up to the planets and stars of the firmament (Phil 2.10). The "god of this age," blinding the minds of unbelievers, tries to frustrate Paul's mission (2 Cor 4.4); the *archontes tou aionos toutou*, astral or cosmic "rulers of this age," have waxed so powerful that they crucified the son of Paul's god (1 Cor 2.8). The *stoicheia*, cosmic astral "elements," once worshiped by Paul's gentiles in Galatia (Gal 4.8–9), and the *daimones* who constitute the "gods of the nations" (1 Cor 10.20–21; cf. Ps 95.5, LXX) are divinities whom Paul's gentiles absolutely must repudiate. These entities may not be "gods by nature" but they still exert a hold on Paul's gentiles and threaten to "enslave" them once again (Gal 4.8–9). To establish the kingdom, the returning Christ will have to defeat these cosmic forces, who will finally acknowledge his sovereignty and that of the Father by "bending knee" whether they are "in heaven," "on earth," or "below the earth" (Phil 2.10–11).[16]

In the meantime, these deities angrily attempt to derail Paul's mission, and they threaten his baptized pagans. Why? Precisely because, as a consequence of receiving Paul's message, these people have abandoned cult to these gods and the pieties traditionally lavished on their images: "Even though there are many so-called gods in heaven or on earth—as in fact there are many gods and many lords—yet for us [that is, for Paul and for his gentiles in Corinth] there is one god, the Father, . . . and one lord, Jesus Christ" (1 Cor 8.5–6; note that Paul does not dispute the existence of these gods, he just urges that they no longer be worshiped). Such a break with their native religions was a nonnegotiable demand of Paul's mission to these gentiles. If a member of the new community lapsed back into his ancestral religious practices, he was to be shunned:

> I wrote to you in my letter not to associate with sexually immoral persons—not at all meaning the immoral of this world, or the greedy, the robbers, or the idolaters—you would need to go out of the world to do so! But I write to you now to say do not associate with anyone who bears the name "brother" [that is, anyone who was a baptized member of the *ekklēsia*] who is sexually immoral or greedy, or who worships idols; a reviler or a drunkard or a robber. *Do not even eat with such a one!* (1 Cor 5.9–11)

In the larger context of the Jewish Diaspora, Paul was unusual in making such a demand. Diaspora communities for centuries before this period and for centuries after encouraged the admiration and the support of their pagan neighbors, and they embraced pagans as patrons of and even as participants in synagogue activities. Outsider affiliation with the diaspora synagogue was ad hoc and voluntary: pagans affiliated *as pagans* while continuing in their native cults as well. Only if a pagan chose to become an "ex-pagan"—that is, if he chose to affiliate with the synagogue community as a *proselutos*, a full "convert"—would he have to repudiate his former gods. Sympathizers, however, did not. The Acts of the Apostles routinely mention such people as "god-fearers"; pagan, Jewish, and later Christian sources also use this term, as well as another: "Judaizers." Both terms are vague, which suits the range of affiliation and activity that they describe. The larger point is the important one: Jews and pagans mixed in the synagogue communities of the Diaspora no less that in the larger religious institution, the ancient pagan city, that was their matrix. As with the temple in Jerusalem (where gentiles had the largest courtyard), so with communities in the Diaspora: Jews made room for pagans *qua* pagans to show respect to the god of Israel.[17]

This practical and stable social arrangement between diaspora synagogue communities and interested pagans drawn from the wider city contrasts sharply with an equally long-lived Hellenistic Jewish rhetorical tradition, one that immediately informs Paul's writings. This rhetoric discoursed lavishly upon the immoral and demeaning consequences of idolatry, defining the pagans' worship of idols as their root sin, and as the root cause of their sin. "How miserable are those, their hopes set on dead things, who give the name 'gods' to the works of human hands," exclaims the author of *Wisdom of Solomon*, sometime in the first century BCE (*Wisdom* 13.10). Such people kill children in their initiation ceremonies and give themselves over to frenzied reveling; they defile their own marriages with adultery, their societies with treacherous murders; they prophesy falsehoods and commit perjury; they lie, cheat and steal (*Wisdom* 14.23–28). We see here, transposed into Greek, the reuse of the old anti-Canaanite biblical polemic, wherein the worship of idols invariably leads to fornication and murder.[18]

Paul the apostle to the gentiles repeats and amplifies *Wisdom*'s themes. Pagans, he says, degrade themselves with passions and with unnatural sexual acts; their minds are debased, their ways malicious, their societies violent, their families distempered (Rm 1.18–32). Paul can be quite pointed in his use of this rhetoric: "Do you not know that wrongdoers will not inherit the kingdom of God? Do not be deceived! Fornicators, idol worshipers, adulterers, homosexuals, thieves, drunkards, revilers, robbers—none of these will inherit the kingdom of God. And such were some of you" (1 Cor 6.9–11). Elements of these Hellenistic "sin lists" characterizing (and caricaturing) pagan culture repeat throughout his correspondence— at 1 Corinthians 5.9–11; 2 Corinthians 12.20–21; Galatians 5.19–21, there as "works of the flesh" ("I am warning you again as I have warned you before: those who do such things will not inherit the kingdom of God!").

For Paul as for the tradition that he draws on, idolatry—the worship of visual representations of lower gods—and idolatry's invariable rhetorical companion, "fornication," are *the* paradigmatic pagan sins. In 1 Corinthians, he emphasizes this teaching by pointing to an episode in Exodus, when Israel long ago had sinned similarly with the Golden Calf:

> Now these things occurred *as examples for us*, so that we might not desire evil as they did. *Do not become idolaters* as some of them did, as it is written: "The people sat down to eat and drink, and they rose up to play" [Ex 32.6]. We must not indulge in fornication [Greek: *porneia*] as they did, and twenty-three thousand fell in a single day. . . .

> These things happened to them to serve as an example,
> *and they were written down to instruct us, upon whom the*
> *end of the ages has come.* . . . Therefore, beloved, flee from
> the worship of idols. (1 Cor 10.6–14)

This is an extraordinary passage. While Paul once again sounds
the trope of the conjoined sins of idol worship and fornication,
he refers them to his own people, Israel, and not to pagans. Why?
In order to summon prestigious Jewish scriptures—"the oracles
of God" as he elsewhere calls them (Rm 3.2)—as the key to
understanding current pagan conditions. (Again, as he says
elsewhere, "Whatever was written in former days was written
for *our* instruction," Rm 15.4; see Rm 4.23–24 for the same
idea.) As a pious Jew, Paul simply assumes the historicity of the
episode of the Golden Calf. But he maintains that scripture preserved the memory of the incident *in writing* precisely in order
to instruct his own contemporary gentile audience, poised as it
was on the cusp of history's great change, the "end of the ages,"
which, says Paul here, has already begun. ("Has come" is past
completed action.[19])

All of Paul's teaching is framed by his conviction that the
kingdom approached. This fact can help to explain his unprecedented demand: not only that "his" gentiles absolutely cease
their worship of idols and of the gods represented by those idols
(a condition otherwise only of full conversion to Judaism), but
also that they *not* "convert" to Judaism (that is, for men, receive
circumcision; Galatians, passim). Why insist that these gentiles
act like Jewish converts, eschewing their own ancestral practices, while at the same time also and heatedly insisting that
they *not* act like converts, honoring Jewish ancestral practices
(circumcision, food laws, and so on)?[20]

Because, as Paul says in Corinthians and elsewhere, the "end of the ages" had already arrived. The turning of the nations to the god of Israel was yet another event anticipated at the End. (We saw this above, briefly, in our passage from Isaiah 2.) Well-represented in biblical prophetic texts—Isaiah 25.6 (Israel and the nations gathered at the temple mount sharing a common meal); Micah 4.1–2 (an echo of our Isaiah passage); and Zechariah 8.23 ("In those days ten men from the nations of every tongue shall take hold of the robe of a Jew, saying 'Let us go with you, for we have heard that God is with you'")—this expectation swells to a major theme in many Jewish writings of the late Second Temple period. Thus the *Psalm of Solomon* expects that at the End, the nations themselves will carry the exiles back to Jerusalem (7.31–41). Repudiating their idols, "all people shall direct their sight to the path of uprightness" (1 *Enoch* 91.14). "All the nations will turn in fear to the Lord God . . . and bury their idols," prophesies *Tobit* (14.6). Note: the word *turning* here does not mean or imply "converting." According to these traditions, the nations do not "become" Jews at the End. In turning to Israel's god, these eschatological gentiles preserve their particular ethnicities as gentiles. They just do not worship idols any more. This is precisely what Paul's gentiles have already done: "You turned to God from idols," he tells the community of Thessalonika, "to serve a living and true god" in advance of the fast-approaching End (1 Thes 1.9–10).[21]

How soon did Paul expect these final events to unwind? "Very soon," is the answer that he gives both early (in 1 Thessalonians, the first letter that we have from him) and late (in Romans, his final extant letter). Paul expects that both he and (most of) his community in Thessalonika will be alive to witness Jesus' second coming, which will trigger the resurrection of the dead and the transformation of the living. "We who are alive," he says there, "we who are left until the coming of the Lord will not precede those who have fallen asleep"—those members of the community, that is, who have died before Christ's return (1 Thes 4.13). "We shall not all sleep" before Christ comes back, Paul says near the finale of 1 Corinthians (15.51). "The appointed time has grown very short" he says at another point in this letter, "the form of this world is passing away" (1 Cor 7.29, 7.31). "Salvation is nearer to us now than when we first believed," he assures gentile Christians in Rome. "The night is far gone, the day is at hand" (Rm 13.11–12).

Jesus of Nazareth, the ultimate source of this message for the Christian movement, had announced the coming kingdom in the late 20s of the first century, and had been executed sometime around the year 30. According to the later gospels, the earliest resurrection appearances began within days of the event. Paul had had his own vision of the risen Christ, scholars calculate, within three years of the disciples' experience—so, circa 33. (See especially 1 Cor 15.3–8.) But those letters from Paul that are preserved in the New Testament probably date to mid-century, some fifteen to twenty years after Paul first had his vision, that much longer since the historical Jesus had proclaimed the nearness of the kingdom. In other words, by the time that Paul dictated his letters—the earliest documents we have from the nascent Christian movement—the kingdom of God was already late.

Whence then Paul's perduring conviction, circa 50 CE, that redemption loomed? Its initial source, according to his own testimony, was that he too had seen the risen Christ, an event that told him—circa 33—what time it was on God's clock. We find him still affirming this interpretation in 1 Corinthians: If Christ has been raised, he says there—and he *has* been raised, Paul insists—then the general resurrection, a definitive end-time event, cannot be far off:

> Now if Christ is proclaimed as raised from the dead, how can some of you say that there is no resurrection of the dead? . . . But in fact Christ has been raised from the dead, the first fruits of those who have fallen asleep. . . . But each in his own order: Christ the first fruits, and then at his [second] coming, those who belong to Christ. Then comes the End, when he hands over the kingdom to God the Father. (1 Cor 15.12–24)

Thus Paul, midcentury. *How had he managed to sustain his conviction of the nearness of the kingdom for almost two decades?* Through the constant reinforcement of his eschatological interpretation of Jesus' resurrection due to the subsequent success of the new movement among pagans. These people—whom Paul refers to quite casually and to their faces as "gentile sinners" (Gal 2.15)—when still worshiping their own gods had been "filled with every kind of wickedness, evil, covetousness and malice. . . . Full of envy, murder, strife, deceit, and craftiness, they are gossips, slanderers, God-haters, insolent, haughty, boastful, inventors of evil, rebellious toward parents. Foolish. Faithless. Heartless. Ruthless" (Rm 1.29–32). It would take a miracle for such people to turn away from their idols—and that is precisely what Paul thought he was witnessing.

Paul's insistence that Christ-following gentiles not be circumcised, in other words, has nothing to do with his personal practice of Jewish ancestral custom, and nothing to do with any supposed antagonism between the *ekklēsia* and the synagogue. Instead, it has everything to do with his vision of the risen

Christ, with his call to be an apostle, and with his sense of his own mission. *The very existence of such gentiles who have turned from their idols and who have made an exclusive commitment to the god of Israel is a profound and ongoing validation of Paul's work.* They confirm him in his conviction that he does, after all, know what time it is on God's clock. They are the reason why he can assert, decades after joining the movement, that "salvation is nearer to us now than when we first believed; the night is far gone, and the day is at hand" (Rm 13.11–12). If he could just bring in their full number, the final events could unwind (Rm 11.25–36). Paul's furious impatience with the circumcisers in Galatia measures the importance of such gentiles to his entire worldview and to his own sense of self. In ceasing to worship their own gods; in calling the god of Israel "*Abba*, Father" and, through the Spirit, becoming God's adopted children (Rm 8.15); and in ceasing to be slaves of sin, Paul's anomalous, exceptional pagans continuously enacted and reenacted this important end-time event, the turning of the nations to Israel's god.

Yet this later iteration of the good news necessarily differed in an important respect from that of Jesus. Jesus' mission proclaiming the kingdom had ended with his execution. His followers, prompted by the vindicating experience of his resurrection, injected a specific, and specifically Christian, innovation into the traditional sequence of end-time events: the messiah, they now held, would have to come not once, but twice. His first coming had been to suffer and die (cf. Lk 24.26). It would be only at his *second* coming—glorious, powerful, leading angelic hosts—that he would raise the dead, gather in the elect, and establish the kingdom of his father (Mk 13.26–27; cf. 1 Thes 4.16–17, recognizably the same tradition, which Paul claims to have "by the word of the Lord").

Final redemption, though near, is nevertheless still in the future, insists Paul, both for the individual whose mortal flesh continues to hold him "a captive to the law of sin" (Rm 7.25) and for the entire universe "groaning and travailing until now" in bondage to decay (Rm 8.22). More than humans must be redeemed: all God's creation awaits. In Paul's view, the very tissue of the cosmos has been rent by sin's power, which abides not only in mortal human flesh but also in the upper spheres of the universe (Rm 8.38). When Christ returns—descending from heaven "with a cry of command and the archangel's call and the sound of the trumpet of God" (1 Thes 4.16)—he will defeat these cosmic powers, rulers and authorities, the lesser deities formerly worshiped by his pagans, and finally he will destroy death itself. Only at that point will Christ "hand over the kingdom to God the Father" (1 Cor 15.24), and God will be "everything in everyone" or "all in all."

How had the entire cosmos, "all creation" (Rm 8.22), heaven and earth, fallen into such dire straits? Paul offers no mythic scaffolding to frame his views, no explanatory narrative of errant angels or of a primeval fall to account for the world's "bondage." He does briefly mention Adam as sin's passageway, through whom "sin came into the world, and through sin, death" (Rm 5.12; cf. 1 Cor 15.20–22, "In Adam all die"). Adam had "trespassed," bringing "condemnation" on himself and on his progeny (Rm 5.18; "By one man many were made sinners," 5.19). Christ, the antitype of Adam and the remedy for Adam's sin, counters—indeed undoes—the "reign of death" begun by Adam. "As one man's trespass led to condemnation for all men, so one man's act of righteousness leads to acquittal and life for all men"; disobedience led to sin, obedience will lead to righteousness (Rm 5.18–19); death will cede to life.

Jesus' death and resurrection, the terminus of his first coming, was redemptive because he died *for* sin (1 Cor 15.3). On account of his sacrifice, the gentile follower of Christ, once baptized, dies *to* sin (Rm 6.2). How so? Baptism "into his death" enables the baptized gentile to "walk in newness of life"—no longer sinful and idolatrous, thus "saved through [Christ] from the wrath of God" (Rm 5.9). What enables him is the "spirit" of God or of Christ that baptism imparts. Through Christ's saving death (which the gentile is "baptized into," Rm 6.3), sin's dominion over the believer is broken and the gentile moves from being sin's slave (when he still worshiped false gods) to being God's slave, a slave to righteousness (Rm 8.9–15). Though still in a mortal, fleshly body ("the body of sin," Rm 6.6), the believer should consider himself "dead to sin and alive to God *in* Christ Jesus. . . . Now that you have been freed from sin and enslaved to God, . . . you have holiness and its goal, eternal life. The wages of sin is death, but the gift of God is eternal life in Christ" (Rm 6.11, 22–23).[22]

Though Romans, like Paul's other letters, is explicitly addressed to gentiles-in-Christ (Rm 1.5–6), Paul also speaks there of sin's universality: "All people, both Jews and Greeks, are under the power of sin" (3.9). When he invokes the effect that law has on sin—enhancing its power (7.7–8), increasing its trespass (presumably, by articulating the offense, 5.20)—it can be hard to tell which population he has in mind: Jews, whose sin is enhanced by the law? Gentiles, who because of idolatry are abandoned to impurity and the indignities of lust (1.18–32)? Both populations "die," the consequence of Adam's sin. On whom does the "law of sin" have such a negative effect?

And readers can be additionally confused by the passage that occurs in the seventh chapter of this rich, and richly convoluted, letter—the morally paralyzed "I":

We know that the law is spiritual, but I am carnal, sold under sin. I do not understand my own actions. For I do not do what I want, but I do the very thing I hate. Now if I do what I do not want, I agree that the law is good. So then it is no longer I, but the sin that dwells within me. For I know that nothing good dwells within me, that is, in my flesh. I can will what is right, but I cannot do it. For I do not do the good I want, but the evil I do not want is what I do. . . . For I delight in the law of God in my inmost self; but I see in my members another law at war with the law of my mind and making me captive to the law of sin, which dwells in my members. Wretched man that I am! Who will deliver me from this body of sin? Thanks be to God though Jesus Christ our Lord! So then I myself serve the law of God with my mind, but with my flesh I serve the law of sin. (Rm 7.14–25)

Who is it that Paul speaks of here? Is he enacting the role of a gentile, lamenting his pre-Christian enslavement to sin? (In Galatians, Paul had spoken of such gentiles who, when they did not know God, were "in bondage to beings that by nature are not gods," 4.8.) Is he speaking of all humans, Jews and pagans both? (Jews, unlike pagans, would be in a position to know "the law of God"—that is, the Torah.) Is Paul then speaking of himself, lamenting his former life as a Pharisee? (This was Augustine's reading, not much followed today. The interpretation runs head-on into Paul's other estimations of himself as an excellent Jew who kept Torah perfectly: "As to righteousness under the Law, I was blameless," Phil 3.6.)[23]

All these interpretations are arguable, and in fact have been argued. But I think that they distract us from the bigger picture. We miss the scope of Paul's vision, and the sweep of his message, if—whether because of his Adam/Christ comparison or his wending description of sin's moral effects in chapter seven— we read "psychologically," focusing too closely on human diffi- culties. Paul thinks big. Not only humankind but all of creation is "subject to futility," caught in the grip of hostile forces. How does Adam's sin affect not only human beings but the whole created cosmos? Whence the malignancy of the "powers"?

Here our modern editions of the New Testament, with their convention of upper- and lowercase letters, can hinder our fol- lowing Paul's argument. When Paul speaks of sin, flesh, and death, we should envisage these as cosmic *agents*: Sin, Flesh, Death. So strong is Sin that it holds everyone, "both Jews and Greeks," in its power (Rm 3.9); so ubiquitous is Sin that it sub- jects the whole universe to its dominion of futility and decay (8.20–22). Working through the Flesh, Sin has even under- mined *ho nomos*, the God-given law, which Paul counts as one of the great privileges of Israel (9.4). "Is the law then sin?" Paul asks rhetorically. And he responds emphatically, *Me genoito!* "By no means!" (7.7). "The law is holy, and the commandment is holy, just, and good" (7.12). "Did that which is good bring death to me? *Me genoito!* . . . The law is spiritual!" (7.13–14). But even the law has been undermined by the cosmic force of Sin; even the law has been "weakened by the flesh" (8.3).

So intimately has Sin woven Death into Flesh that the fleshly body itself, precisely because it *is* fleshly, cannot be redeemed. Only Christ can deliver the sinner from "this body of death" (Rm 7.24). For this reason, Paul had taught that "Flesh and blood *cannot* inherit the kingdom of God, nor does the perish- able inherit the imperishable" (1 Cor 15.50). At the resurrec- tion, the dead rise and the living are saved through a radical transformation, through which the body of flesh, quick or dead, transmutes from a physical body to a *soma pneumatikon*, a spiritual body; no longer mortal, but like the body of the risen Christ (1 Cor 15.24). In the meantime, "all of creation groans," awaiting its redemption (Rm 8.23).[24]

What, then, is the mechanism of this redemption? How does Christ's death by these hostile cosmic powers work to effect a universal salvation? On this issue Paul mobilizes the language of sanctuary, sacrifice, purity, and holiness—the language, in other words, of the Jerusalem temple. Christ serves as *the* sacrifice par excellence. But what sort of sacrifice? Here Paul is less than clear. His reference to Christ as a Paschal lamb in 1 Corinthians 5.7 is, upon examination, less descriptive than hortatory: in that passage, Paul urges his gentile followers to cleanse themselves of the "leaven" of pride in view of the fact that the (metaphorical) holiday of Passover is already underway. The Paschal image, in other words, refers to Jewish timekeeping (leaven should be long gone by the beginning of Passover!), not to a sacrificial death on the part of Christ. (And Paschal offerings, in any case, are not "for sin.") On the other hand, 2 Corinthians 5.21 and Romans 8.3 do present Christ forthrightly as a "sin sacrifice," but this also seems confusing: sin sacrifices did not cleanse the sinner, but the sancta of the temple. The *hilasterion* of Romans 3.25, finally, is a sacrifice of expiation; but again, the image is extremely confusing (and, I think, confused): In Leviticus, penitent humans bring the offering (16.6–22); in Romans, it is God who brings Jesus. The closest analogy to a sacrifice in Paul's time that would bear away the sinner's sin would be the scapegoat of Yom Kippur (Lv 16.21). But Paul nowhere uses this image and, besides—a nod to the eucharistic traditions—no one eats scapegoats. In brief, to present Christ's death as a sacrifice, Paul falls back on the wellsprings of his tradition—Genesis, Exodus, Leviticus, Numbers, and Deuteronomy—but no single biblical paradigm controls the metaphor.[25]

By comparison, Paul's language of "sanctification" with respect to his pagans-in-Christ, and his representations of his own work as "priestly service" (*hierourgounta*, "priest-work") are surprisingly clear, as is his reference to the rituals at Jerusalem's altar that serve as his template. His Thessalonian gentiles, for example, in turning from their idols to the living and true god, have attained *hagiasmos*. Where the Revised Standard Version translates "sanctification," we should equally understand "separation" or "dedication": the distinction between what was "common" (*hol/koinos* in the Hebrew and Greek, respectively) and what "dedicated to God" (*kadosh/hagios*) was fundamental to the ritual protocols of Jewish sacrifice. Only that which was both pure (or "clean") and holy (or "separated out" from the common) was fit to be brought to God's altar. Paul's Thessalonians, now knowing God and amending their ritual and sexual behavior, are separated out or distinguished from those other gentiles, the idolatrous ones who do *not* know God (1 Thes 4.4–5). Those who do know God have been called "not to impurity"—the moral consequence of idolatry and porneia—but "in holiness" (4.7). Elsewhere, Paul simply refers to these ex-pagan pagans as "holy ones" (RSV: "saints," Rm 1.7; 1 Cor 1.2). These people have been made "holy"—separated out, dedicated to God—by God, through baptism and spirit, in Christ (1 Cor 1.2). Through this language of purity and sanctification, in other words, Paul transforms his *gentiles* into a now acceptable sacrifice, with himself as the one who helps with the offering: through God's grace, Paul serves as a "priest's assistant"—*leitourgos*, the septuagintal translation for "Levite"—"sacrificing the gospel of God," bringing his gentiles as a sanctified offering to Jerusalem (Rm 15.16; cf. 12.1, where he exhorts these gentiles to regard their own bodies as a living, sanctified *thusia*, a "sacrifice dedicated to God"). In brief: Paul uses the language of the Septuagint's sacrificial cult to characterize the ways that Christ—who serves in Paul's metaphorical web as priest/*cohen* to Paul's Levite—binds the gentiles into the sweep of Israel's impending redemption.[26]

Elsewhere, Paul presents the sanctification of his gentiles by analogy to the temple itself. These people, like God's temple, are filled with God's spirit: "Don't you know that you are God's temple, for God's spirit dwells in you? . . . For God's temple is holy, and you are that temple" (1 Cor 3.16); "Your body is a temple of the holy spirit" (1 Cor. 6.19); "We are the temple of the living god" (2 Cor 6.16). Fornication and idol worship, accordingly, have no place in that community/*ekklēsia*, whose members are already "washed" (thus made "clean") and "separated" from the common or the profane ("sanctified," *hagiasthate*, 1 Cor 6.17)—now speaking of the gentiles both as God's temple and as a sacrifice suitable to it. Baptism "into" Jesus' death, in both these instances—gentiles as offering, gentiles as temple—is the means by which Paul's gentiles receive *pneuma*, spirit.

New Testament scholars will sometimes point to these verses by way of arguing that, for Paul, Jerusalem's temple has been superseded by this new, spiritual "temple" of the Christian community. The opposite seems more likely to me: Paul praises the new community by likening it to something that he values supremely. Had he valued the temple less, he would not have used it to exemplify his communities; if he had challenged the function and probity of the laws of sacrifice, he would not have used them as the binding metaphor for his mission. For Paul, God's spirit dwells *both* in Jerusalem's temple *and* in the "new temple" of the believer and of the community. (See, again, Romans 9.4, where *doxa*, "glory," refers specifically to God's glorious presence in the temple; for a similar conviction attributed to Jesus, see Matthew 23.21.) Put otherwise: the Eucharist, for Paul, does not replace, displace or contest the sacrifices made to God by Jews in Jerusalem's temple. For Paul's gentiles-in-Christ in the Diaspora, however, the Eucharist replaces and in some sense annuls their former sacrifices to false gods.

Sin's scope is universal for Paul. It permeates the cosmos; it defines the human (but especially the pagan) condition. The repair of the cosmos would come only with the turning of the age, when Jesus as triumphant returning messiah would subdue the hostile powers, then "hand over the kingdom to God the Father" (1 Cor 15.24–28; Phil 2.10–11, with its assortment of more-than-human "knees," implies their same chastened acknowledgment). Christ's death as sin sacrifice, and spirit-giving baptism into his death, releases some small portion of humanity now. (In Romans, Paul will refer to this portion as a "remnant . . . chosen by grace" when he designates Jews [11.5], and as "those who have attained righteousness" when he refers to baptized gentiles [8.30].) And then at the End, to the sound of the heavenly trumpet, the returning Christ will descend "with a cry of command" (1 Thes 4.16) to triumph once for all over Sin, Flesh, and Death.

Yet what of the rest of humanity? What, specifically, of the huge majority of pagans still worshiping their gods, who will be the object of God's "coming wrath" (1 Thes 1.10; Rm 1.18)? What of the "unbelievers in Judea" (Rm 15.31) and the great majority of Israel, ignorant of or indifferent or hostile to the *euangelion* (Rm 11.5)?

About the pagans Paul seems oddly nonchalant. In his final letter, written perhaps from Corinth, he announces his plans to travel to Rome, then on to Spain, saying simply, "I no longer have any place [for the gentile mission] in these regions" (Rm 15.23). He continues,

> In Christ Jesus, I have reason to be proud of my work for God. I will not venture to speak of anything but what Christ has wrought through me, to win obedience from the gentiles by word and by deed, by the signs of powers and wonders, by the power of the holy spirit, so that from Jerusalem as far round as Illyricum I have preached the gospel of Christ fully, though trying earnestly not to preach the gospel where Christ has already been named, in order not to build on a foundation laid by someone else. (Rm 15.18–20)

All of these regions, from the eastern Mediterranean to Asia Minor, have not suddenly become Christian. It is difficult, then, to know what Paul means by this statement, except perhaps that he feels crowded, and that he can be more useful in Spain. But if he is convinced, as he states in Romans, that "salvation is nearer to us than when we first believed; the night is far gone, the day is at hand" (13.12), what does he expect will happen to all these pagans?

And what about the rest of "the Jews"? On this question Pauline scholarship has undergone a seismic shift since the 1970s. The ruling paradigm had been (and with slight modifications, alas, still is) that Paul, in becoming an apostle of Christ, repudiated temple and Torah, replaced law with grace, condemned circumcision, and conceived his gentile communities as a "new Israel" or as "the Israel of God" (Gal 6.16). Only those Jews who agreed with Paul, who likewise repudiated the law, and who also joined the new Christian movement—so goes this interpretation—would be "saved." In this view, in other words, Christianity as a gentile religion distinct from and hostile to Judaism was already fully born in the first generation of the new movement.

Yet when scholars began to attend more to both Paul's intense eschatology and his explicit focus on gentiles, perspective shifted, and so did interpretation of his letters. Paul's fury in Galatians, for example, is directed not toward Jews in general, or toward Judaism in general, but toward competing Christian missionaries who advocate circumcising Paul's gentiles-in-Christ. He repudiates their position as profoundly wrongheaded, misconstruing as it does (he urges) what God had wrought through Christ for gentiles, in conformity with his ancient promise to Abraham: in Abraham "all the gentiles will be blessed" (Gal 3.8; Gen 12.3). If the gentiles are all made to "become" Jews through conversion/receiving circumcision, they will *not* "be" gentiles any more, thereby nullifying the promise (Gal 3.17): "For if inheritance comes from the Law, it no longer comes from the promise. But God granted it to Abraham through the promise!" (Gal 3.18). Paul accordingly does not oppose circumcision tout court—that is, for Jews or for Jews-in-Christ; in fact, no such topic is addressed in this or in any other letter. Rather, Paul opposes circumcision for gentiles-in-Christ. In this newer scenario, surprisingly, it is Paul who emerges as a Jewishly traditional figure, his circumcising competitors the radical innovators. Neither in quotidian circumstances nor in eschatological traditions did Jews practice or anticipate "missionizing" gentiles to turn them "into" Jews.[27]

So also with Paul's sarcasm and anger in 2 Corinthians 10–11. Other missionaries—Jews in the Jesus movement, like Paul himself—had moved into Corinth and challenged Paul's authority: "Are they Hebrews? So am I. Are they Israelites? So am

I. Are they descendants of Abraham? So am I. Are they servants of Christ? . . . I am a better one" (2 Cor 11.22–23). Paul's harshest condemnation of "Jews," in other words, is directed to those Jews who are fellow apostles. Perhaps also his experience with these competing apostles who intrude, in his view, into his own communities is what informs Paul's own sensitivity about "not building on another's foundation," which he explicitly disavows doing (Rm 15.20).

So also, finally, with "the law." Instead of insisting that Paul saw the Torah as a "fleshly" encumbrance having no place in the new movement, scholars began to pay attention to the complexity of Paul's usages. The "law of sin" at work in the flesh, for example, is clearly other than and opposed to "the law of God" (Rm 7.21–25). "Do we overthrow the law by this faith?" he rhetorically asks his gentile readers in Rome. "Of course not! On the contrary, we uphold the law" (Rm 3.31). "This faith" refers to verses 21–30. In this reading, verse 28—"We hold that a person is justified by faith [i.e., faith in Christ's sacrifice] apart from the works of the law"—refers to gentiles-in-Christ, and *not* to humanity in general. And throughout his letters, Paul grounds his authority in his reading of the "law and the prophets." He urges his gentiles to "fulfill the law" (meaning, specifically, the Ten Commandments; Rm 13.8–10). Further, by insisting that his gentiles absolutely relinquish cult to their native gods, Paul demands that they enact publically the single behavior that majority culture, and Jews themselves, universally and exclusively associated with Jews.[28]

This new perspective on Paul has profoundly affected how scholars now read Romans, especially chapters 9–11. Paul in these chapters addresses the ultimate fate not only of all the "unchurched" pagans, but also of "my own people, my kinsmen"—that is, non-Christian Jews. To do so, he audaciously rereads the Bible.

Paul begins by confessing his "great anguish and sorrow" for his kinsmen. After blessing God for the privileges that he has bestowed upon Israel—their family status as his children, the glorious divine presence in Jerusalem's temple (reduced to just "glory" in most English translations!), the covenants, the giving of the Torah, the temple cult [often translated bloodlessly as "the worship"], the promises, the patriarchs, and the messiah (Rm 9.4–5)—Paul proceeds to draw a distinction between "Israelites" and "Israel": "Not all Israelites truly belong to Israel, and not all of Abraham's children are his true descendants." Paul then narrates a rapid sketch of Israel's history encompassing Genesis, Exodus, and the prophets, pointing out those times when God, for his own sovereign reasons, has directed that history. Not all of Abraham's children were Israel, only those through Isaac; nor all of Isaac's children, but only Jacob, not Esau, a decision God made before they had been born. (Why? So that "God's purpose of election might continue," Rm 9.11.) Is God unjust in doing so? Paul asks rhetorically ("Of course not!" 9.14), next alluding to God's hardening of Pharaoh's heart. God can have mercy on whomever he wants, and he can harden whomever he wants, because he's God, who explained to Pharaoh, "I have raised you up for the very purpose of showing my power in you, *so that my name may be proclaimed in all the earth*" (9.17). Nodding toward Isaiah and Jeremiah, Paul continues: God is the potter and humanity the pots, all made from the same lump of clay. God can make whatever kind of pots he wants: "Who are you, O man, to argue with God?" (9.19–25). This review sweeps into Paul's lament for his people, who cause Paul "great sorrow and unceasing anguish"(9.2); in the words of Isaiah, God will "save" only a remnant of Israel (9.27).

Romans chapter 9 had set a plumb line in older, traditional interpretations of Paul, constraining the reading of the rest of the letter: those Jews like Paul who "have faith" are the "saved remnant"; the ones who do not have faith "have stumbled" and will not be saved until and unless they change (9.27). Most of Israel, says Paul, are unenlightened, insubordinate to God's plan, uncomprehending, disobedient (10.1–21). Things look bad for the (non-Christian) Jews.

If the letter ended here, this older interpretation—that Paul thinks that everybody, Jew and gentile, has to be "Christian" to be saved—would be more compelling. But the letter does not end here. Paul's argument surges ahead in chapter 11, where he puts the question at its most pointed: "Has God then rejected his people?" The question, again, is rhetorical ("Of course not!" 11.1). God "has not rejected his people whom he foreknew." He works by freely choosing a remnant for himself. "So too *at the present time* there is a remnant, chosen by grace" (11.5; Paul had pointed to himself as obviously a member of this group, 11.1): chosenness means election (11.7). What of all the rest of Israel? They are hardened, but it is *God who hardened them* (11.7–10).

Why? Paul's language here resonates with his earlier reference to the story of Pharaoh (Rm 9.17). Once again, God has "hardened" someone—in this case, most of Israel—for the same reason that he had once hardened Pharaoh: so "that my name may be proclaimed in all the earth." When will his name be so proclaimed? When his son returns (11.26), when the kingdom comes—which means, for Paul, very soon: "If their being cast off means the reconciliation of the *cosmos*, what will their reception mean, if not life from the dead!" (11.15, obviously a reference to impending end-time events). In his excitement Paul continues, mixing metaphors (foot races, dough, olive trees) as he tries to explain God's plan. Israel is still very much in "the race." Their divinely induced "stumbling" did not disqualify them (11.11); rather, it was God's strategy in order to bring "riches to the gentiles"—namely, salvation in Christ (11.12). The part of the dough that a Jew brings to God is holy, and it sanctifies all of the dough (an allusion to offering first fruits to priests, 11.16). The root and the trunk of the cultivated olive are still holy, even if some branches have been knocked off to make room for wild olive grafts (11.17–24; Do not boast about this, he cautions his gentile hearers: the knocked-off "Jewish" branches will be grafted back into the tree.) Paul then comes to his point:

> I do not want you to be ignorant of this *musterion*, brothers, lest you think that you are wise. A hardening has come upon part of Israel, until the *pleroma* of the gentiles comes in, so that *all of Israel will be saved*, as it is written: "Out of Zion will come the Deliverer; he will banish ungodliness from Jacob. And this will be my covenant with them, when I take away their sins." (Rm 11.25–27)[29]

For the time being, Israel is the "enemy of the gospel" for the sake of the gentiles. (Most English translations, unconscionably, render this phrase as "enemies of God," but Paul's Greek has no such construction: he nowhere mentions "God" here, 11.28.) But Israel's election was never in doubt, their status as "beloved" always secure. This is because Israel—all Israel—rests upon the promises that God made long ago to Abraham,

Isaac, and Jacob, "the fathers," and God is constant, his promises sure. *"The gifts and the calling of God are irrevocable,"* Paul asserts, and

> Just as you [gentiles] were once disobedient to God but now have received mercy through their disobedience, so they, now disobedient, may receive mercy now on account of the mercy shown you. *For God has imprisoned all in disobedience, so that he may show mercy to all.* (Rm 11.30–31)

At the thought of this universal redemption, Paul breaks out in praise:

> O the depth of the riches and wisdom and knowledge of God! How inscrutable his judgments, how unsearchable his paths! For who has known the mind of the Lord? Who has been his counselor? Who has given him a gift in order to receive a gift back from him? From him and through him and to him are all things. Glory to him forever! (Rm 11.33–36)

From this peak statement of happy conviction, Paul moves into instructions on behavior to the Roman community: love and support one another, and bless those who persecute you (Romans 12); respect state authorities, pay taxes; love your neighbor in order to fulfill the law (a nod to Leviticus 19.18), and do not act like idol-worshiping gentiles (no "reveling and drunkenness, debauchery and licentiousness, quarreling and jealousy," Romans 13.13). Do not be judgmental about who eats what: community is what matters (Romans 14). Then, heading toward his conclusion, Paul summons once again the authority of Jewish scripture, "written in former days for *our* instruction, so that through the steadfastness and encouragement of the scriptures, we may have hope" (Rm 15.4). In one deft sentence he then sums up the argument of chapters 9 to 11: "Christ became a servant to the circumcision [Israel] in order to show God's truthfulness, to confirm the promises that he made to Abraham, Isaac and Jacob [regarding the redemption of Israel], and so that the gentiles would glorify God for his mercy" (15.8). Paul then chants a catena of biblical verses that celebrate the gentiles' turning to God, their worshiping together with Israel, and their subordination to God's messiah (the "root of Jesse," 15.12). He ends his letter with the image of (baptized) gentiles as the sanctified sacrifice that he will bring to Jerusalem.

So what happens with all those other, unbaptized pagans, in Paul's view? And what happens with his unpersuaded kinsmen, Israel *extra ecclesiam*? Romans 11.25–26 holds our answer. In this brief caesura in normal time, the moment between Christ's resurrection and his second coming, says Paul, only a remnant of Israel and only a fraction of gentiles have received the good news that the kingdom is on its way. Understanding the Bible's transparency on current events, these groups live by hope. Ethnically distinct—Jews are Jews, and gentiles, Paul insists, should remain gentiles and not convert to Judaism—these two peoples are gathered together in this eschatological moment into the *ekklēsia*, working signs and wonders, prophesying, healing (more evidence, like their eschewing idols, that these "eschatological" gentiles, like their "eschatological" Jewish colleagues, are filled with God's spirit).

God's hardening of (most of) Israel to the message of impending redemption is temporary and providential. He will cease when his purpose has finally been achieved, when his name has been proclaimed on all the earth. Then the "full measure" or "full number" or "fullness"—*pleroma*—of the nations will "come in," and "so all Israel will be saved" (11.26). But when is this moment? He continues, quoting Isaiah, "Out of Zion will come the Deliverer" who will take away Israel's sins (11.26–27). Again, when? That, Paul asserts, is a *musterion*, a divine mystery (11.25). The redeemer from Zion refers to Jesus' second coming as messiah: Paul expects this to occur from Jerusalem. The hour of that event is unknown and unknowable: as Paul says elsewhere, "The day of the Lord will come like a thief in the night" (1 Thes 5.2). But it comes soon.

Paul's clauses in this passage twist into a tight knot: What sequence of these events does he foresee? First the gentiles "come in," then "all Israel," then the second coming? First Christ returns, initiating the incoming of those pagans who so far had been outside of the gospel, and then "all Israel"? Sequential? Simultaneous? This is a *musterion*, after all.[30]

Yet Paul's vision of redemption is no less commodious than are the older Jewish apocalyptic traditions upon which he draws, wherein all the nations turn to Israel's god and all Israel is gathered in when the day of the Lord finally dawns. The peculiarities of the Jesus movement—the message of a messiah who had died and been raised before establishing the kingdom—had called into existence this double loop in the sequence of saving events. Instead of the messiah's coming, then Israel's redemption, then the turning of the nations, as more classical patterns had it, Paul sees two comings of the messiah, the election of some within Israel and some of the gentiles, and then, eschatologically, a second messianic appearance bringing together the rest of Israel and the rest of the nations. Paul improvises. Scripture provides his sheet music here, but the urgency of the times, between the resurrection and the second coming, compels his stunning variations. And the main theme of his theological cadenza sounds clearly: God sent his son to die in order to redeem the world from sin—or, rather, from Sin, and from all the other rebel cosmic forces ranged between God and his creation. "If God is for us," Paul proclaims to the gentile Christ-followers in Rome, "who is against us?"

> He who did not spare his own son but gave him up for us all, will he not also give us all things with him? . . . Who will separate us from the love of Christ? Shall tribulation? Or distress? Or persecution, or famine, or peril, or nakedness, or the sword? . . . No, in all these things we are more than conquerors through him who loved us. For I am certain that neither death, nor life, nor angels, nor principalities, nor things present, nor things to come, nor powers, nor height, nor depth, *nor anything else in all creation* will be able to separate us from the love of God in Christ Jesus our Lord. (Romans 8.31–39).

Paul thus envisages a divine comedy, a cosmic happy ending. And he—like John the Baptizer and like Jesus before him—is convinced that these events will happen *soon.*

Yet the kingdom did not come, though traditions established by these three men continued. What happened then to Paul's message, to their message, when Time failed to end on time?

Chapter 2
FLESH AND THE DEVIL

Sin in the Second Century

Both Jesus and Paul, despite their very different audiences, constructed their respective ideas about sin, and about redemption from sin, from within a common biblical heritage. Sin as violation of the covenant (for Jews); sin's remedy as repentance, prayer, immersion (thus, purification); sacrifice: teachings that we can reconstruct from the synoptic gospel materials place Jesus securely within the world of late Second Temple Judaism. Sin as idolatry with all its attendant violations of decency (for pagans), sin's remedy as a commitment to worship the god of Israel alone, and to live by the behavioral standards that such a commitment implies: teachings that we can cull from Paul's letters place Paul securely within the world of Late Second Temple apocalyptic hope. The earliest stirrings of what would become Christianity are incontrovertibly—even idiosyncratically—Jewish.

But Paul's world was not Jesus' world. His biblical tradition was Greek, not Aramaic or Hebrew. His rhetorical education and the imagined architecture of his cosmos were incontrovertibly pagan. This had real advantages during his lifetime: Paul could communicate passionately and persuasively across ethnic lines with his gentile communities. (Not that he could not be misunderstood: on the evidence of his own complaints, not infrequently he was.) And this also had real advantages for Paul's continuing importance *after* his lifetime, in terms of his rich reinterpretability (and misinterpretability). His rhetoric, and the cosmic architecture implied in his letters, continued to resonate with later audiences long after his urgent eschatological conviction, due to the simple force majeure of time, proved impossible to maintain.

Paul stretched his time-driven gospel over the spatial frame provided by antiquity's map of the cosmos. Inherited from Aristotle and the Hellenistic astronomers, this map placed the earth at the center of the universe. Around the earth, in ascending degrees of perfection, revolved the seven spheres of the moon, the sun, and the five known planets. Beyond these, higher still—highest in terms of beauty, perfection, and stability—the luminous sphere of the fixed stars marked off the utmost edge of the visible universe. Conscious, intelligent, these celestial beings in their ordered ranks were commonly regarded (by Jews no less than by pagans) as themselves divine. In his commentary on Genesis, Philo of Alexandria, a Hellenistic Jewish philosopher and elder contemporary of Paul's, refers to these beings as *theoi*, "gods." According to Philo, the heavenly firmament was "the most holy dwelling-place of the manifest and visible gods" (*On the Creation of the World* 7.27). When Paul speaks of the "god of this world" (2 Cor 4.4), or of the *archontes, exousiai,* and *dunameis* ("rulers," "authorities," and "powers," cf.1 Cor 2.8, 15.24); when he warns his gentile communities not to enslave themselves again to the cosmic "elements" (*stoicheia,* Gal 4.8–9) nor to eat at the "table of demons" (1 Cor 10.21); when he acknowledges that "there are many gods and many lords" (1 Cor 8.5) it is these beings, inter alia, that he has in mind.[1]

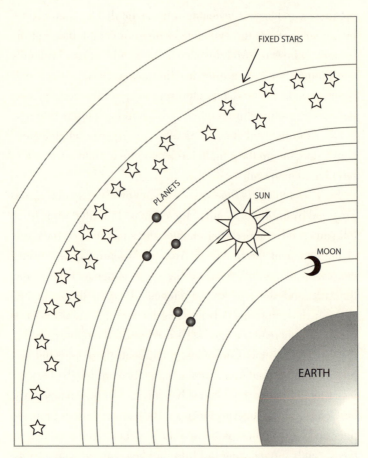

Figure 2. Illustration of the Ptolemaic cosmos. The Jewish philosopher Philo of
Alexandria, in his commentary on the book of Genesis, remarks that the heavenly
firmament was "the most holy dwelling-place of the manifest and visible gods" (*On the
Creation of the World* 7.27). These celestial divinities, since they have visible bodies,
are "lower" and lesser than the god of Israel, who for Philo is acorporeal, the highest
god and the source of all else in creation. The geocentric architecture of the Hellenistic cosmos, in other words, encoded moral value: what was "up" was "good"—"better"
both metaphysically and morally than what was "down." The apostle Paul charges
this picture of the physical universe with apocalyptic polarities: astral and cosmic
"elements" (*stoicheia*, Gal 4.3) represent the demonic gods formerly and wrongly
worshiped by his baptized gentiles, entities to be subdued by the returning triumphant
Christ at his second coming (1 Cor 15.24; cf. Phil 2.10–11). Some two centuries after
Paul, Origen would invoke the consequences of sin as the fundamental cause of this
structure of the physical universe.

Those forms of Greco-Roman high culture that owed most to Plato could see in this god-congested universe the trace of a single high divinity, "the One" or "the Father," or, simply, *ho theos*, "the god," who was the world's ultimate source. Radically transcendent, perfect, changeless, good, without body of any sort whatsoever (since body implied limit), this god could be "seen" only with the mind. At or as the god's opposite (and notional) extreme was *hulē*, coeternal unformed matter: defective, radically unstable, mutable, utterly without form. "Between" them, the result of their "interaction," the visible cosmos stood. To the degree that the cosmos was beautiful, well-ordered, rational, and good it reflected the attributes of the high god. To the degree that the cosmos was subject to movement and change it expressed the consequences of its unstable material substratum. The higher up in the cosmos, the greater the beauty and stability of the spheres; the lower in the cosmos, the greater the degree of movement and change. Below the moon, conditions deteriorated rapidly. Matter grew thick, balky, and sinister; chance, change, and fate ruled life on earth.[2]

Though the high god was the ultimate source of *kosmos*— the word itself means "order"—he was not its creator. That function would have compromised his perfection, involving him in change. The organization of the cosmos accordingly devolved to a lower deity, variously described as a "craftsman" (*demiourgos*) or as the "world ruler" (*kosmokrator*) or as "divine reason" (*Logos*). When Paul teaches that Christ was God's preexistent agent in creation, "through whom all things are" (1 Cor 8.6), or when the Gospel of John presents Christ as God's Logos "through whom all things came into being"(Jn 1.1–3), they speak from within this system. Lower still were those deities attached to stars and planets. Divinities could also be local to places on earth (sacred springs, caves, or mountains), and they presided over the well-being of certain cities (for example, Athena for Athens, Diana for Ephesus, Aphrodite for Aphrodisias, and so on). They attached also, to peoples, particular ethnic groups: in antiquity, gods no less than humans were "ethnic." (The Jews were odd in this regard, claiming both that their god was ethnic, the "god of Israel" who presided over Jewish history, *and* insisting that he was the lord of the entire universe. We will see shortly how intellectual Christian gentiles will interpret this claim.) Other ethnic gods, the "gods of the nations," said the Greek translation of a psalm, were "demons," meaning "lower gods" (*daimones*, Ps 95.5, LXX). These "lower gods" could also be referred to as *angeloi*, the root of our word "angels." They served as messengers between heaven and earth.[3]

All of these many divine personalities were native to ancient monotheism, the view that beneath the myriad levels and manifestations of divinity in the cosmos stood a single absolute source. Ancient monotheism, in other words, addressed the issue of heaven's architecture, not its absolute population. As long as one god stood at the absolute apex of holiness and power, pagan, Jewish, and eventually Christian monotheists could and did accommodate vast numbers of lesser deities ranging beneath.[4]

These lesser gods buffered the serenely distant high god from the busyness of celestial and terrestrial life. And these divine intermediaries, like matter itself, served a vital apologetic function, providing a ready theodicy, an explanation for the existence of evil that did not compromise the absolute goodness of the high god. If and when bad things happened—and bad things accumulated rapidly in the realm below the moon—these lesser cosmic forces, or the lability and liabilities of matter itself, could account for them. The stately order of the upper spheres corresponded to and reflected their closer relationship

to the high god, the chaos and evils of earth to the capricious-
ness of lower gods and to the instability of recalcitrant sublunar
matter.

Human architecture echoed cosmic architecture. Like the
universe, the human being was a composite of higher and lower

Figure 3. Mosaic zodiac from Beit Alpha synagogue. Ancient monotheism encom-
passed a multiplicity of gods. As long as a single high god stood at the pinnacle of
holiness and power, any number of lesser deities could range beneath. The zodiac
itself was an ecumenical road map of reality, invoked in pagan, Jewish, and Christian
art and architecture. Valentinian Christians, according to Clement of Alexandria,
associated the twelve apostles with "the twelve signs of the zodiac. For just as birth
is regulated by them [that is, by the astral deities], so is *re*birth directed by the
apostles," (*Excerpts from Theodotos* XXV, 1). On the floor of their synagogue in late
Roman Palestine, Jews depicted this wheel of the heavens rotating around the chariot
of the sun god, Helios. Courtesy Granger Collection/Alinari Archives.

aspects: a fleshly body animated by a lower soul, which humans shared with animals; and a higher part of soul, the vessel or docking point of "spirit" or "mind" (the soul's "eye"). The higher, rational part of the human shared a fellowship with the stars, those sensible expressions of eternal beauty, and it was to the realm of the stars—specifically, to the Milky Way—that the souls of the good, after shedding the fleshly body, might repair after death. The lower, nonrational parts of the human, the soul subject to passion that joined spirit to physical flesh, remained where it was native, in the sublunar realm.[5]

The dipoles of this cosmic architecture also echoed within the binary opposites that shaped *paideia*, high Greek educational culture: philosophical speculation, rhetoric, and literary theory. The One/the many; intelligible (seen with mind)/sensible (perceived through the senses); spirit/matter; soul/body: these dipoles not only shaped the universe, they coded values. Spirit was "better" than matter not only metaphysically but also morally; and the temptation to see the lower term as "bad" because the upper term so obviously was "good" inhered in this system itself. However, such a move held dangers. It could slide into impiety, calling into question the absoluteness of the high god. (If he were all good and all-powerful, why his involvement, albeit attenuated, with so derelict a medium as matter?) And it could compromise ethics. (If one's soul erred because one's fleshly body was "bad," what room or role remained for free will? Paul's rhetorical convolutions about sin, flesh, spirit, and law in chapter 7 of Romans well illustrate the problem.)

Philosophers might try to avoid such polarized thinking, but rhetoricians positively embraced it. Constructing argument through sharp contrasts gave speech beauty, ancient grammarians taught. And if, in forensic argument, one could urge the audience that one's opponents were *completely* bad, one's own position impeccable—indeed, the only position that any right-thinking person could embrace—well, what was the point of argument, if not persuasion? (Paul's fulminations against his competition in Galatia showcase this sort of rhetoric.[6])

Finally, the very approach taken by the thoughtful reader who sought meaning in texts was shaped by the structures presupposed by cosmology's antipodes. The obvious meaning of a text, the narrative immediately available to even the most simple reader, corresponded to its "body" or "flesh." But beneath or above this obvious level lay the inner, spiritual, or hidden meaning, one that pointed to higher truths. All sorts of reading strategies suggested ways to wrest the truths that a text might hold from what it simply said. Ancient thinkers with commitments both to high philosophical culture and to inherited, traditional narratives about divinity ingeniously resolved the tensions that could result by developing various "spiritual" understandings of their literatures.

The worse the text in communicating responsible, respectable information about the divine, the clearer was its invitation to the pious and well-educated reader to search out its *huponoia*, its "undersense." Thus Sallustius, a fourth-century CE pagan Platonist, who wrote:

> That the myths are divine can be seen by those who have used them—inspired poets, the best philosophers, and the gods themselves in oracles. . . . But why do they contain stories of adultery, robbery, father-binding, and all the other absurdity? Is it not perhaps a thing worthy of admiration, done so that by means of the visible absurdity the Soul may immediately feel that the words are veils, and believe the Truth to be a mystery?" (*On the Gods and the Cosmos* III)

Similarly, and for similar reason, Philo of Alexandria in the first century had defended the opening narrative in his Bible:

> Now these [stories in Genesis 2–3] are no mythical fictions such as the poets and sophists delight in. Rather, they are modes of making ideas visible, bidding us to resort to allegorical interpretation. (*On the Creation of the World* 56.157)

Drawing correspondences among cosmos, text, human intelligence, and ancient anthropology, the great Christian scholar Origen of Alexandria summed up these reading techniques as a pedagogical principle:

> The simple man should be edified by what we may call the "flesh" of scripture, that is, its obvious interpretation; while the man who has made some progress may be edified by its "soul," as it were; and the man who is *teleios* ["mature" or "perfect"] may be edified by the spiritual law. For just as man consists of body, soul, and spirit, so in the same way does scripture. (*On First Principles* 4.2, 4; cf. 1 Cor 2.6–7)

A "fleshy" man simply could not grasp a text's highest, spiritual meanings; to speak spatially, such a man was stuck in the realm below the moon, where "flesh" was native. The spiritual man, however, read at a "high" level: for him, a sacred text was a window opening onto eternity.

This is the cultural context within which we must interpret an odd claim that lies buried in two late New Testament texts, a claim that attests to a certain level of education on the part of some late first-century/early second-century Christians. In a group of writings known as the Johannine epistles, the author warns his audience to beware of some other Christians:

> Beloved, do not believe every spirit, but test the spirits to see whether they are of God; for many false prophets have gone out into the world. By this you shall know the spirit [that is] of God: every spirit that confesses that *Jesus Christ has come in the flesh* is of God, and every spirit which does not [so] confess Jesus is not of God. (1 Jn 4.1–2)

> [Jesus Christ] came by water and *blood*, not with the water only but with the water and the *blood*. (1 Jn 5.6)

> Many deceivers have gone out into the world, men who will not acknowledge *the coming of Jesus Christ in the flesh*. Such a one is the Deceiver and the Antichrist. (2 Jn 7)

We know next to nothing about these repudiated Christians. But their claim that Jesus had not had a fleshly body made eminent sense. It cohered with and supported another assertion—made as early as we have our earliest evidence, Paul's letters—that Jesus was God's divine preexistent agent in creation, his demiurge or (per the Fourth Gospel) his Logos (see p. 53).

Paul, mid-first century, had made very high claims for Jesus as God's son. Before Christ appeared "in the form [*morpha*] of a slave, coming in the likeness [*homoiomati*] of human beings, being found in the fashion [*schemati*] of a human," Paul says, Christ had been "in the form [*en morphai*] of God," not deeming it robbery to be *isa theou*, "equivalent to God" (Phil 2.6–8). Translation of this passage is difficult. Four centuries after Paul's lifetime, councils of the imperial church will declare that

Christ is "fully God"—that is, as divine as God the Father. But Paul does not seem to claim the same here: the whole passage presents God as Christ's superior. Christ obeys God, Christ is humbled to the point of death, God is the one who lifts Christ up high, God is the one who is finally "glorified" (2.9–11). Clearly, however, Christ is the divine entity closest to God.

Putting aside the question of Christ's degree of divinity— Paul clearly does consider Christ to be a god, here and elsewhere in his letters—this difficult passage raises another: how human did Paul imagine Christ to be? Those Greek words that I have emphasized speak of similarity or surface appearance ("form," "shape"). "Looking as if he were human" would capture their tone. So, similarly, "For God has done what the law, weakened by the flesh, could not do: sending his own son *in the likeness* [again, *homoiomati*] of sinful flesh and as a sin offering [or: on account of sin], he condemned sin in the flesh" (Rm 8.3). This last verse compounds the problem of Christ's in-flesh-ness. Not only is human flesh (like the animal flesh that it is) bounded by the orbit of the moon, but such flesh, Paul says here, is also sinful. If flesh is too lowly to be brought into intimate connection with divinity, *sinful* flesh—the type of flesh that dies; mortal flesh (Rm 7.24)—is that much less appropriate, even nonsensical. By the coordinates of Greco-Roman paideia, the higher Christ's divinity, the harder to imagine him enfleshed.

Yet Paul speaks elsewhere and easily of Christ's "blood" and of Christ's "death," terms that certainly strongly imply that his body was mortal, thus normally human. And Paul's Christ is "born of woman" (Gal 4.4), descended from David "according to the flesh" (Rm 1.4). So what did he mean? The best that we can conclude, I think, is the obvious: when Paul speaks of Christ, whether of some aspects of Christ's divinity or of his humanity, he speaks neither categorically nor consistently. A mid-first century Jewish apocalyptic visionary, Paul was not burdened by an obligation to frame a systematic and coherent Christology in the way that later theologians will be. He proclaims his gospel in order to prepare his audiences for the rapidly approaching kingdom.

Later readers of his letters, however, were by definition in a different situation. The kingdom had tarried. Foundational traditions from the first generation of the movement had to be reinterpreted to remain meaningful. We know that by the late first and early second centuries, collections of Paul's correspondence were circulating. And we know that they confused people. "There are some things in them that are hard to understand," warned a second- or third-generation pseudepigraphic author, "which the ignorant and unstable twist to their own destruction" (2 Pt 3.16).[7]

Had those Christians repudiated in the Johannine correspondence read Paul? We cannot know. But the position that John condemns them for—claiming that Christ had not had a fleshly body—could certainly find support in Paul's letters. Modern scholars call their position *docetism*, from the Greek verb "to appear" (*dokein*): docetic Christology is "appearance" Christology. The position worked well within the rhetorical binary opposites through which Paul built his arguments: spiritual/carnal, grace and spirit/sin and flesh, spirit and life/flesh and death. And it cohered effortlessly with antiquity's map of the universe.

Other binary pairs also shaped Paul's letters: contrasts between gospel and law, between grace and the "works of the law," between Greek and Jew, between the uncircumcised and the circumcised. Gentile forms of Christianity as they developed in the course of the second century polarized these pairs: gospel, grace, uncircumcised, and Greek were "good"; law, works of the law, circumcision, and Jew were "bad." A very surprising turn in military events and imperial politics, further exerted a tremendous influence on such polarized readings, validating and reinforcing them. In 70 CE, after a long and bloody Jewish uprising, Rome smashed Judea and utterly destroyed the temple in Jerusalem. Some six decades later, in 132, Judea again erupted in revolt. By 135, Jerusalem itself was erased; and over its ruins Hadrian built a new, pagan city, Aelia Capitolina. Altars to Roman deities now smoked on the blasted plain where once the temple had stood. The gods of Rome had defeated the god of the Jews.[8]

What effect did all of these factors—cosmological, anthropological, rhetorical, political—have on evolving Christian ideas of sin?

~~~~

Before we can explore the second century of Christianity, we must glance ahead to events in the fourth. In 312 CE, toward the end of a brief, brutal struggle between military strongmen in the Western Roman Empire, a victorious Constantine began Christianity's conversion to a form of late Roman imperial culture. He threw his prestige, his authority, and a good deal of publicly funded largesse behind one sect of the church, in effect empowering its bishops to suppress their rivals. Thus began a new stage in the empire's persecution of Christians, this time pursued by Christians themselves. By the end of the fourth century, the bishops' battle against Christian diversity had resulted in a practical victory for the "orthodox" church (that is, for the church now supported by the state).

Their victory affected not only the future but also the past. By banning the texts of "deviant" Christians, burning their books or simply impeding their being copied, the bishops got to remake the Christian past in their own image: the only documents to survive were the ones that they approved. This ancient triage consigned countless gospels, apocryphal acts, sermons, prayers, letters, liturgies, commentaries, and theological treatises to the ash heap of history. The record of the Christian past, in short, was effaced by the church itself.

The victors' muscular retrojection of fourth-century definitions of orthodoxy compromises our view of developments in the second century, a period of particularly rich Christian diversity. To map only a small area of this very varied terrain, I propose to triangulate using the work of three major second-century theologians. Two of these three were so important and influential in their own lifetimes, and established such vital, widespread and long-lived communities then and thereafter, that their writings, vigorously repudiated by other Christian contemporaries, were eventually suppressed by their fourth-century orthodox opponents—in the case of one of these theologians, with complete success.

In light of how much united all three of them, this acrimony can seem surprising. The intellectual commitments of all three depended upon points of principle drawn from pagan paideia. All three applied these principles to orient themselves within the enormous written patrimony of western Judaism, the Septuagint. And all three had to make sense of those traditions from and about Jesus, and from Paul, in light of the destruction of Jerusalem and the necessity of reinterpreting the intense eschatological expectation proclaimed in those first-century texts.

Their high god, further, was not the lord of Jewish history but the supreme deity of pagan philosophy: unique, changeless, perfect, radically transcendent; and for all three, this perfect deity was the father of Jesus Christ. All three asserted, in light of their commitment to this idea of the high god, that the divine intelligence organizing the material cosmos could only be a lower god. And all three concurred that this lower god was the creative deity described in Genesis and active throughout the Septuagint. Finally, all three held that the Septuagint, interpreted "correctly"—that is, with spiritual understanding—provided fundamental insight into Christian revelation.[9]

These deep areas of agreement notwithstanding, broad scope for argument remained. By comparing the work of these three contemporaries—Valentinus (fl. 130), Marcion (fl. 140), and Justin Martyr (fl. 150)—we will gain a view of the ways that new gentile communities made sense of their common Jewish heritage, constructed their own Christian identities, and interpreted ideas of redemption and, thus, of sin.[10]

~~~~~~

Valentinus and Valentinian Christianity were easier to describe when scholars knew less. Dependent on the hostile witness of proto-orthodox writers—Irenaeus, Hippolytus, Tertullian, whose works by and large survived the fourth-century triage—modern academic descriptions more-or-less echoed the ideas given in these ancient ecclesiastical ones. Thus, the Alexandrian Valentinus, rejected by the proto-orthodox Roman church, went on to found his own movement, which was a Christianized form of Gnosticism. Gnosticism itself was a theosophical and radically dualistic form of religion that mixed elements from Platonism, apocalyptic Judaism, and other more oriental forms of mythology. These Gnostics were radical dualists: they believed in two gods—a high god, previously unknown before the revelation of Jesus Christ, and a lower, malevolent god, the god of the Jews, who was the author of matter. Accordingly, they depreciated not only the Jewish god but also the Jewish books, which they subjected to fantastic interpretations. Among these interpretations was their elaborate myth of a precosmic fall of divine wisdom (*Sophia* in Greek), whose disoriented wanderings inadvertently gave rise to the creator god of Genesis. This material cosmos, in brief, was fundamentally the product of a disastrous accident. Accordingly, Christ when he did appear in the lower material realm did not actually possess a body of flesh, since matter was the creation of the evil god. Rather, he was a phantasm, a sort of optical illusion, only seeming to possess a lowly body. This docetic Christ never suffered or died; he merely seemed to.

Salvation from the alien material realm depended upon the esoteric knowledge brought by Christ and communicated secretly to his disciples. Only "spiritual" men (*pneumatikoi*), those humans with a sufficient degree of the divine spark within them, could receive such knowledge; for others it was difficult if not impossible. This was so because humanity reflected the cosmic order: some people were *sarkikoi* or *hulikoi*, "fleshy" or "material," and utterly incapable of salvation. The *psuchikoi*, "soulish" people, could receive some knowledge, but they were limited by their very natures in how far they could advance. Only the *pneumatikoi* were truly and fully saved, and they were saved on account of their nature: the Gnostics, rigidly deterministic, disavowed any scope for free will. Finally, Gnostic ethics could take one of two extreme forms. Many Gnostics were strict ascetics, attenuating involvement with matter through fasting, celibacy, and mortification of the flesh. But others, drawing on this same notion of alienation from the lower realm, were notorious profligates, infamous for their orgies and sexual immorality.[11]

With the discovery (in 1948) and publication (in the 1970s) of the Nag Hammadi Library, which included a number of fourth-century Coptic translations of mid-second-century Greek

Valentinian texts, scholars no longer had to rely solely on hostile
heresiology as their point of departure for reconstructing Valentinus and his church. Interpretation (as we will shortly see) has
shifted. Unfortunately, no such spectacular find has come to the
aid of understanding Marcion: all his writings are lost. For his
work, we still depend on statements made and fragments preserved in the polemics of his enemies.[12]

Thus, in 140, Marcion, well-educated and wealthy, moved
from his native Pontus, by the Black Sea, to Rome. By 144, the
Roman church had excommunicated him for his heretical ideas.
Marcion, like the Gnostics, taught the doctrine of two gods and
a docetic Christ. But whereas the Valentinians had come to this
view by drawing on a huge and eclectic assemblage of books—
the Septuagint (especially Genesis), various gospels, apostolic
letters and apocalypses, and a considerable number of their own
inspired writings—Marcion derived his doctrine almost exclusively from the letters of Paul. Reading the contrasting pairs
that shaped Paul's rhetoric as polarized opposites, Marcion concluded that law and gospel, flesh and spirit, Jew and gentile
pointed to two different moral and cosmic domains. The creator
god of Genesis and the chief deity of the Septuagint was the god
of the Jews. The god of the gospel, the redeemer god, unknown
until the revelation of Christ, was the god of the Christians.

From this constellation of theological positions Marcion dis-
tilled a completely unprecedented scriptural lesson. The Septuagint, he concluded, as a Jewish book should be left to the
Jews. Those scriptures spoke of a military messiah and of an
ingathering of Israel back to Jerusalem. Writing in the wake of
Judea's two disastrous revolts against Rome, Marcion could
point to the obvious: such a messiah, manifestly, had yet to
come. For the [gentile] Christian, the *only* texts that were holy

scripture should be a new collection, which Marcion proceeded to produce: a gathering of ten Pauline letters and a version of the Gospel of Luke. These, he said, had been corrupted by Judaizers (hence the places in them where Paul inconsistently seemed to praise the law, or where Luke had seemingly tied the figure of Christ to the prophets of the Jewish god). Marcion accordingly expurgated these passages—or, in his view, restored these texts—thereby producing a de-Judaized scripture, a "new" testament.[13]

The figures of Valentinus and Marcion have long been shrouded by the thick haze of ancient antiheretical rhetoric. Historians have become more aware of the implications of that rhetoric, however, as the field of comparative ancient religions has developed over the past forty years. For example, scholars now question the analytic utility of such terms as *Gnostic* (especially as regards Valentinus) or *heretical*. Both terms rely upon ideas of "true religion" as pure, unmixed, chronologically prior, and so on—the self-claim of the heresiologists for their own communities, condemning rival Christian communities as their moral and doctrinal opposites. Heated polemic rarely yields reliable description.[14]

The stories told about both Valentinus' and Marcion's rejection by the Roman church, evaluated in this light, while remaining good rhetoric, are most likely bad history: in the second century, there was no "orthodoxy" in Rome or anywhere else, just a wide variety of different communities, all of which represented differing trajectories developing over the course of time and none of which exercised a generally recognized authority. From the moment that we have writings from what will eventually become Christianity—that is, with Paul's letters, circa 50—we have evidence of energetic diversity. Put differently, there never was a time (for that matter, not even after the ascent of Constantine) when a single interpretation of Christianity prevailed. Put a third way, in the early second century, there was no such thing as "the" church. Put a fourth way, *all* forms of second-century Christianity differ from *any* form of the first-century movement, not least of all because of the necessary adjustments to eschatology called forth by the simple passage of time.

Sexualized slander was also common coin of ancient rhetoric. The accusations enabled the accuser to construct an idealized self-portrait as he leveled the charge of profligacy against "the other." Ethnic difference, gender difference, doctrinal difference: all could be and were constructed by imputing sexual deviance and promiscuity to the "not-self." (We have already seen how the Hellenistic Jewish authors of *Wisdom* and of the New Testament's letter to the Romans used this trope when constructing "rhetorical pagans," pp. 25–27.) When modern historians portray "heretics" as sexual libertines, they repeat ancient calumnies; they do not give historical description.[15]

With these caveats in mind, how are we to gauge the ideas of sin that shaped these lost Christian communities? We know from a Valentinian text, Ptolemy's *Letter to Flora*, that the Ten Commandments were valued as "pure legislation unmixed with evil . . . which the Savior came not to destroy but to fulfill—for that which he fulfilled was not alien to him" (*Letter to Flora* V, 1). This law was ordained by "the Demiurge and Maker of this entire universe and of what is in it" (VII, 4), a god of justice who, if distinct from the high god who is the father of the savior, is nonetheless also distinct from the adversary, the devil (III, 2; VII, 3). The moral status of matter in itself is thus not the fundamental cause of evil, nor are the Jewish scriptures disavowed as positive sources of moral instruction.

Looking at Valentinian views of Christ—specifically, of how and from what Christ as savior saves—is another way to track these concepts of sin. On this issue, patristic descriptions of (or complaints about) "docetic" Christology can be extremely misleading. Heresiologists deploy that rhetoric in order to highlight what *they* thought was essential to redemption, namely, the sacrificial aspects of Christ's flesh and blood. "Docetism" set up their chief charge: if Christ did not have real human flesh, then his crucifixion was a "fraud," the so-called resurrection a trick, and so on. (Tertullian, in his treatise *On the Flesh of Christ*, provides a pitch-perfect example of this sort of polemical argument.) To the proto-orthodox, a Christ without human flesh meant a Christ who could not function as a sacrifice, thus a Christ who did not redeem. (Tertullian, again: *Against Marcion* 3.9.) But Valentinus, when speaking of Christ's body, emphasizes its "continence" and "divinity": since "he did not possess corruptibility," Jesus "ate and drank in a special way, without evacuating food. So great was his power of continence that the food was not corrupted in him" (*Excerpts from Theodotos* LIX, 3). Valentinus here emphasizes the *moral* quality of Jesus' body, which in turn is expressed physiologically. And more fundamentally, for Valentinus it is Christ's message and the knowledge of the divine Father that he brings, not his bodily medium as such, that matters for Christian redemption.

Valentinus' root metaphors for constructing salvation in and through Christ differ from the ones used by his proto-orthodox critics. From what does Christ save? From sin, surely; but this is presented in *The Gospel of Truth* as error (or, rather, as "Error": in this gospel, the cosmos experiences emotional and intellectual states, which are personified). The Pleroma (a spiritual region, on which more below), though it proceeds from the Father, is ignorant of him. From this ignorance arises a febrile

disorientation: Fear, Terror "like a dense fog," Error, Forgetfulness (XVII, 5–10). Error is the source of forgetting and fear
(XVII, 30); it (or she; the Greek word *Planē* is feminine) leads
some people to sin (XXXII, 35). Jesus came to enlighten those
in the dark of Forgetfulness, thereby angering Error, which (or
who) nailed Jesus to a cross/a tree (XVIII, 20).

At exactly this point, Valentinus' gospel brings together an
astonishing range of associations: references to the tree of
knowledge in the garden of Eden, to the cross of Christ, to the
Christian Eucharist, to the principles of late Platonic ethics and
epistemology. The agency of "Error," for example, narrativizes
a point of Platonic ethics: misdeeds are mistakes, caused by not
knowing or thinking "correctly," according to what is, in the
most profound sense, true. And an ultimate goal of the philosopher within this tradition is self-knowledge, Socrates' famous
instruction *gnothi seauton,* "Know thyself." (Error cannot know
herself: coming into being in a fog, ignorant of the Father, she
has no "root," XVII, 30). Refracting gospel tradition, Valentinus describes Jesus as crucified by Error. Jesus thereby serves
not as a sacrifice, but as "the fruit of the knowledge of the Father" (XVIII, 20–25): the cross becomes Eden's tree. By eating
of Jesus/the fruit of the tree of the crucified/the Eucharist, the
Christian gains saving knowledge of the Father, which brings
truth, light, perfection.

Valentinus, in brief, turns the more familiar readings of Genesis 3 and of the Passion narratives on their heads. Whereas in
those readings Adam and Eve's eating of the tree's fruit is history's first sin, punished by suffering and death, and Christ's
crucifixion is the ultimate act of religious malfeasance, ultimately punished by the temple's destruction, Valentinus sees
things differently. By being "nailed to a tree" Jesus becomes

"the fruit of the knowledge of the Father" while also bringing to those who partake of this fruit/of himself the revelation of their true identity, too. One can know God only through Christ, and can know herself only through knowing God and Christ:

> [The fruit/Jesus] did not cause ruin because it was eaten. Rather for those who ate of it, it gave the possibility that whoever he discovered within himself might be joyful in the discovery of him. And as for him, they discovered him within them—the inconceivable, the incomprehensible, the Father, the Perfect One who created the *[P]leroma* . (*Gospel of Truth* XVIII, 25–35)[16]

Ignorance of the Father thus seems not culpable in and of itself, but it does lead to sin. Valentinus, as we have seen, conceives this ignorance not merely on a human scale but also on a cosmic one, thereby catching as well an important dimension of Paul's message. The word that I left untranslated in italics above, *Pleroma*, means "fullness" or "the all." For Valentinus it indicates an immaterial, spiritual region, an invisible heaven above the visible heavens, whose ultimate source is, again, the Father. In this, too, we see the ways that Valentinus narrativizes certain Platonic ideas. In Platonism, the lower, material world— the world where humans dwell—is an inferior image of the spiritual world, an upper immaterial world of ideas, which is its source. What is invisible is real; what is visible (embodied, material) is, by comparison, unreal. To state the same idea differently, for Plato, the One—purely transcendent and immaterial—is superior to and precedes the many (the material world). *Gospel of Truth* relates these principles through its story. Events or situations in the (spiritual, upper) Pleroma correspond to events or situations in the human world: in both, Error acts; ignorance of the Father, thick as fog, causes fear and anxiety; Christ is crucified by mistake; his eucharistic manifestation conveys redemptive knowledge. Ultimately, both the "aeons" above (those entities/mental states populating the Pleroma) and the human believer below, freed from the disturbances of ignorance, are gathered up into the unity of knowledge, to the One (XXV, 1–XXVIII, 1).[17]

Who are these aeons? For a fuller answer, we must turn to those fragments from Valentinus and his followers preserved by proto-orthodox heresiologists. According to Irenaeus, the aeons of the Valentinian Pleroma proceeded from the One in linked male-female pairs ("syzygies," as in the modern Hebrew *zug*, a "couple"; Greek nouns, like French or German ones, have gender; English does not). Thus depth (*Bythos*, a masculine noun) linked with Silence (*Sige*, a feminine noun) together formed the first gendered pair to emanate from the Father. From them in turn another sygygy emanated, *Nous* and *Aletheia* ("Mind" and "Truth"), who in turn produced *Logos* and *Zoe* ("Life"), and so on: these ideas or entities or mental states give the Pleroma its complex structure (Irenaeus, *Against Heresies*, I.1, 1–I.2, 2).

The last or youngest of the female aeons produced was Sophia, ("wisdom"). She conceived a passion to know the Father more intimately than she could, and it drove her to wander from her proper place in the Pleroma, seeking him:

> This passion is said to be the search after the Father, for she wished . . . to comprehend his greatness. Since she was unable to do this, . . . she was in very deep distress,

because of the greatness of the depth of the unfathomable-
ness of the Father and because of her love for him.

Encountering Limit (*Horos*, also personified as an active agent),
Sophia renounced "her original purpose, together with the passion that had arisen from her stupefied wonder" (*Against Heresies* I.2, 2). Chastened, she returned to her proper place with her
proper "consort" (I.2, 4).[18]

Sophia's fall has cosmic consequences. Ultimately, she is responsible for the generation of a lower deity, the Demiurge, who
in turn creates the lower, material world (*Against Heresies* I.5,
1–4). Both this god and his creation are related to the upper
world, but as distorted or defective images of it. It is here, in
this lower world, that people themselves struggle (as had Sophia) with the disorienting afflictions of ignorance and passion.
These last, again, do not seem to be sinful in and of themselves,
even though they result from a "fall"; rather, they are a condition that inhibits knowledge of God. Renouncing passion—for
the believer no less than for this errant aeon—is the first step
back to restoration and unity. According to Theodotos, a follower of Valentinus, "the Savior came down to tear us away from
the passions and to bring us into union with himself" (*Excerpts
from Theodotos* LXVII, 4).[19]

What about Marcion's views on sin? Here we have only
such clues as remain in the massive refutation of his work, the
five books of Tertullian's hefty *Adversus Marcionem*. In this
treatise, Tertullian's silences are as significant as are the
themes that he does sound. Despite the routine rhetoric of
abuse leveled at the ethics of Christian competitors, for instance—that seeming ascetics were actually libertines, or that
docetic Christology undermined the entire idea of salvation in

Christ—"not even Tertullian can find any strictures to pass on the morals of Marcion or his adherents," whose ethic of celibacy and of heroic martyrdom even the "orthodox" grudgingly acknowledged.[20]

The best that Tertullian can do is complain that Marcion's (commendable) ethics seem logically inconsistent with his separation of law from gospel (1.19). Why live ethically, he complains, why avoid sin, if you don't believe that God punishes sinners? It's all well and good to love God, but can you really love God if you do not also fear him? The Marcionites, Tertullian observes, refuse to impute to the high god, the father of Jesus, "those emotions of mind which they object to in the Creator. For if he displays neither hostility nor wrath, if he neither condemns nor judges, how stable can his moral law be?" (1.26). But if that were the case, "how shall you love," he challenges, "unless you fear not to love? . . . If you decline to fear your god because he is good, what keeps you from bubbling over into all manner of vice? . . . Why during persecution do you not at once offer your incense?" (1.27).

To these questions, Tertullian notes with exasperation, Marcionite Christians answer "*Absit, absit!*" The standard modern English edition of this work translates their exclamation as, "Oh no, far from it!" That misses its Pauline resonance. The Latin *absit*, in this connection, translates Paul's Greek exclamation, *Me genoito*, which means something like, "God forbid!"

Is God unjust to inflict wrath on us? *Me genoito!* (Rm 3.5–6)

Should we continue in sin so that grace might abound? *Me genoito!* (Rm 6.1–2)

Should we sin because we are not under Law but under grace? *Me genoito*! (Rm 6.15)

I ask then, has God rejected his people? *Me genoito*! (Rm 11.1)

Tertullian's badgering questions (insinuations, really, and that's the best that he can do) echo one half of the argument that Paul had presented in Romans chapters 5 and 6: does dying to sin—the effect of baptism into Christ—make sinning alright? With Paul, Marcion answers, if sharing in eternal life with Jesus means that we have died to sin, this means as well that we now control our fleshly passions. We have become "slaves to righteousness" (Rm 6, passim).[21]

To conclude our brief review of these two suppressed theologians, I return to the first of our earlier questions: how did these second-century gentile thinkers make sense of their common first-century Jewish legacy? In some ways, Valentinus and Marcion preserved this legacy similarly. Both saw Christ ("the messiah") as the agent of the high god. Both regarded ethics as conforming to the will of the high god. Both eschewed honoring pagan deities with cult, a behavior that, before the first generation of what would become Christianity, was associated universally and exclusively with Judaism. They saw the high god and his son as actively committed to the project of human redemption. Both men defined sin in ways that resonate with the Ten Commandments, with Matthew's Sermon on the Mount, and with Pauline moral instruction. All of these points of principle we could deem "Judaizing," and both men, Valentinus and Marcion, hold them together (mutatis mutandis) with Jesus of Nazareth and with Paul.

In other ways, of course, these two theologians subject their Jewish legacy to radical revision. Each drops the first generation's eschatological clarion call. For them, redemption is not temporal, bodily, and communal so much as spatial, spiritual, and individual, an ascent of the saved believer's true self or spirit out of the lower cosmos to a realm above. (Shorn of his eschatology, Paul's comment in 1 Corinthians 15.50—"Flesh and blood cannot inherit the kingdom of God"—obliges them here.) Neither associates their high god with the god of Jewish scripture. In keeping with Mediterranean antiquity's common-sense association of particular gods with particular ethnic groups, Marcion sees the god of Genesis, the god worshiped by Jews in Jerusalem, not as some sort of universal deity but rather (and sensibly enough) as the god of the Jews; Valentinus sees him as a cosmic accident, the inadvertent divine product of Sophia's cast-off passion. Therefore, each concludes, this demiurgic deity was *not* the father of the messiah/Christ. And both sever the Septuagint from a directly positive relation to their gospel—Valentinus by exegesis, Marcion by "de-Judaizing" Paul's letters and his version of Luke's gospel, by presenting this new collection of texts as specifically Christian scripture, and by relinquishing the Septuagint to the Jews.

What about their respective Christian identities? How do Valentinus and Marcion construct these? Orthodoxy's complete destruction of Marcion's writings makes any definitive answer to this question elusive. From Tertullian's polemic, we can safely surmise only that Marcion drew heavily on Paul—again, minus Paul's vivid eschatology—and that he consistently delineated law from gospel, as he took Paul to have done. Paul's original message, as we have seen, had been heavily "ethnic": he had founded his gospel in no small part on his understanding of God's promise to Abraham, on his reading of Israel's prophets, on his view of the irrevocable election of Israel, and on his principled maintenance of the distinction between Jews and pagans/gentiles, both of whom would be gathered in, distinct but together, at the final, universal redemption. (See pp. 27–28.) In the opposite direction, Marcion's gospel was no less ethnic, too. De-Judaizing his gospel and Paul's letters, relinquishing any connection between Israel's scriptures and the Christian message of salvation, he rendered his church an explicitly "gentile" enterprise. Presumably, any Jews wanting to join his church would have to abandon their ancestral texts and practices, much as Marcion most likely imagined Paul to have done.

Yet in striking contrast both to some strains of Gnostic Christian tradition preserved in the Nag Hammadi Library and to all known genres of proto-orthodoxy and of orthodoxy from the second century up through the twenty-first, Marcion's de-Judaizing of the gospel does not seem to have led him to delegitimize or demean Judaism. The Jews' covenant with their own god, he taught, remained. Jews understood their own scriptures correctly: they rightly awaited the coming of their own messiah, who would gather in their nation and reestablish a Jewish kingdom in Judea (*Against Marcion* 4.6). Judaism was for the Jews; the message of Jesus and of Paul, however, was for the salvation of gentiles. Marcion, in brief, seems not to have used "Jew" as an antitype by which to sharpen his definition of "Christian."[22]

The Valentinian construction of Christian identity drew on Paul's legacy in different ways. For them as for Marcion, the contrasting "other" by means of which they articulated their own sense of self was not the Jews. Rather, they distinguished themselves and their church from those who were "material" (*hulikoi*) or "fleshy" (*sarkikoi*) who, according to Paul, were not able to receive "the secret and hidden wisdom of God" in the way that the "perfect" (*teleioi*) or the "spiritual" (*pneumatikoi*) could do (1 Cor 2.6–3.3). The "soulish" (*psuchikos*) person might also have difficulty discerning spiritual truths (2.14), but she stood in a middling position between the extremes of *pneuma* and *sarx* or *hyle*: she could be worked with. This tripartite scheme corresponded to the makeup of an individual person (composed of spirit, soul, and fleshly body), to constitutive categories of the cosmos, and even to the levels of meaning available in a single text. (So Origen, quoted on p. 58.) The particular ethnic identity of the obdurately reprobate—pagans? Jews? certain non-Valentinian Christians?—was subordinate to their diagnostic label: such people were caught up in fleshy, material, lower ways of being, thinking, and acting. They would never ascend to the realm above, free of the flesh, to which the pneumatic or psychic Christian could aspire.[23]

For both Valentinus and Marcion, then, sin was an action contrary to divine will and a state of being separated from the high god, of living *kata sarka*, "according to the flesh." *Flesh* as a constitutive element both of the human being and of the lower cosmos stood in their discourse as shorthand for sin, for ignorance, for every mortiferous state of being that opposed the redemption available through Christ. Life *in the flesh* was the fate of all humanity dwelling in the sublunar realm; but by receiving divine spirit through baptism, by learning the will of the Father through the revelation of his Son, by reading sacred texts with spiritual understanding, the Christian could mitigate this terrible situation. The gospel enabled the baptized Christian to live *kata pneuma*, "according to spirit," despite still living in the fleshly body until, shedding that moral and mental encumbrance at death, she could bypass the planetary spheres and the hostile rulers of this age and ascend to the realm of the Father. "Salvation" for both Valentinians and Marcionites meant redemption *from* the flesh.

For the proto-orthodox, however, salvation meant redemption *of* the flesh. From this point of principle, all else followed: the way that they construed their Jewish heritage, the way that they constructed their Christian identity, the way that they understood sin and redemption. We can see how this was so by examining the work of Valentinus' and Marcion's younger contemporary, Justin Martyr.

"That which always maintains the same nature," asserts Justin, conjuring the by now familiar features of philosophy's supreme deity, "in the same manner, and is the cause of all other things—that, indeed, is god" (*Dialogue with Trypho* 3). For him as much as for Valentinus and Marcion, this god by definition could not possibly be the busy divinity so active throughout the Jewish Bible. Who was it, then, who spoke to Moses out of the burning bush? Who appeared to Abraham at Mamre, and later to Jacob? "All the Jews even now teach that the nameless god spoke to Moses!" Justin, with irritation, observes (1 *Apology* 63). Arguing the same point with Trypho, he comments, "Even the least intelligent person would never assert that the Maker and Father of all things, quitting affairs above the heavens, was visible on a small corner of earth" (*Trypho* 60). Clearly, the Septuagint's divine protagonist had to be a *heteros theos*—another, lower god (*Trypho* 56). How then does one discern the true identity of this Jewish god? Again with Valentinus and Marcion, Justin answers, by interpreting the scriptures with spiritual understanding. But Justin's reading produces an answer different from theirs. The god of Abraham, Isaac, and Jacob, he concludes, the god who showed up throughout Jewish history, is the *son* of the high god, Christ before his incarnation (1 *Apology* 63; cf. *Trypho* 38; 56–62).

This interpretation initiates a radical reinterpretation of Jewish scripture. Before we explore what Justin changes, however, we should note what he keeps. First, by preserving a positive connection between the high god and the Bible, as opposed to the contrasting relation that Valentinus and Marcion had each introduced, Justin affirms a position more like Paul's own. So too with his insistence that Jesus was the messiah promised in Jewish scripture; Paul would agree. Justin denounces idolatry as drastically wrong in terms that would have been immediately familiar to any of his Jewish contemporaries. And finally, Justin's views on the nature and even on the venue of final redemption—we will look at some details shortly—resonate even more closely with traditions of Jewish eschatological expectations than did Paul's own.

Justin is an apologist for his community, which he defines in terms drawn from (pagan) philosophy. Wrong intellectual concepts of God, such as those displayed by pagan philosophers, result in bad human behavior: license in speaking, acting howsoever one chooses, indifference to doing evil (*Trypho* 1). Christians committed to Justin's version of Christianity, by contrast, are chaste, prudent, pious, good citizens—all virtues traditionally ascribed to "good" philosophers. Sin occurs when someone does something "contrary to right reason" (*Trypho* 141): intellectual error precedes moral error. And with a flourish, Justin urges that any pagan philosophers who ever said something true (such as Socrates or Plato) were actually beholden to the preincarnate Christ, God's Logos in the world: "Whatever things were rightly said among all men are the property of us Christians" (2 *Apology* 13; cf. 7 and 10). Justin's Christianity, in brief, is the true philosophy.[24]

But Justin asserts his community's identity in a field filled with challengers: other Christians, hostile pagans, skeptical

Jews. He lambastes each while championing his own identity by dwelling on the sins of these others. An earlier Jewish tradition helps him to frame his critique: the story of the fallen angels of Genesis 6.1–4 and their demonic progeny, the gods of the nations (cf. Ps 95.5, LXX). These divine powers, Justin maintains, assist rival Christians, deceive pagans, and seduce Jews.[25]

Justin identifies members of churches other than his own as "atheists, impious, unrighteous and sinful, confessors of Jesus in name only . . . yet they style themselves 'Christians'!" They in fact are much like gentile idol worshippers, who indulge in nefarious and impious rites. He continues, "Some are called Marcians, some Valentinians . . . others by other names," identified by the originator of their particular opinions, much as pagan schools of philosophy are (*Trypho* 35; cf. 2). "Some who are called Christians, but who are actually godless and impious heretics," he continues, "teach doctrines that are in every way blasphemous, atheistic and foolish." (Justin cites as a case in point those false Christians who blaspheme the god of Abraham, Isaac and Jacob, who say there is no resurrection of the dead, and who think that their souls, when they die, ascend to heaven.) These people are to be strictly distinguished from true Christians, such as Justin and those of his community, who are "right-minded" (*Trypho* 80). How then does Justin account for the success of these other groups? Demonic agency. Marcion, in particular, "a man of Pontus who is even at this day alive . . . by the aid of demons has caused many of every nation to speak blasphemies" (1 *Apology* 26; see also 58). Pride and poor thinking inaugurate heresies; demonic forces then propel them. Sin, especially that of blasphemy, is the invariable and obvious result; fornication, cannibalism, and secret, lurid nocturnal rites, Justin suggests, lurk covertly (1 *Apology* 26).

What of pagans? On this topic, Justin embroiders older Jewish stories about the "fallen angels" of Genesis 6. These celestial
powers, after wrongly breeding with human women, produced
demons; they then went on to subdue humanity through magic,
through fear and punishment, and by teaching people to offer
sacrifice, incense, and libations "of which things they stood in
need after they were enslaved by lustful passions." Not content
to stop there, these beings and their demonic offspring then
"sowed murders, wars, adulteries, intemperate deeds, and all
wickedness," deceiving poets and mythologists, who mistook
these supernatural beings for gods (2 *Apology* 5). The son of the
high god entered human history accordingly "for the sake of be-
lieving men, and for the destruction of demons": Christian exor-
cism alone beats these creatures back (2 *Apology* 6). In response,
the demons retaliate by instigating pagan anti-Christian perse-
cutions (2 *Apology* 13). For this sin, both of these "races," divine
and human, will justly be held accountable, Justin warns, because God created both species rational, thus with free will: their
doing evil is their own choice (2 *Apology* 7; cf. 1 *Apology* 28).

For Justin as for the Jewish traditions that he draws on, the
paradigmatic pagan sin is the worship of false gods and their
images—a theme strongly present in Paul's letters as well. The
synoptic gospels, by contrast, their stories set within the predominantly Jewish context of Galilee and Judea, had relatively
little to say about or against paganism. "Jewish" sins—a breaking of the terms of the covenant between God and Israel—dom-
inate their narratives, as do exhortations to live according to the
commandments (see pp. 15–17). In those rare places where the
evangelists' Jesus does encounter a pagan (the Gerasene demo-
niac of Mark 5 and parallels, the Syro-Phoenician woman in
Mark 7 and Matthew 16, Pontius Pilate in all of the Passion
narratives), a surprising delicacy prevails: no mention is made

of the person's paganism. And in Acts, part 2 of Luke's gospel, the author similarly tiptoes around idolatry, not mentioning the paganism of the Ethiopian eunuch (assuming that this character is envisaged as a god-fearer and not a proselyte, Acts 8.27–28), nor that of the god-fearers attached to synagogues both in Judea (the Roman centurion Cornelius, Acts 10.1–2) and routinely elsewhere (e.g., in Pisidian Antioch, Acts 13.16; in Philippi, 16.14; in Thessalonika, 17.4; in Corinth, 18.7).[26]

The theme of the pagan worship of idols and false gods sounds in Luke's story only once the narrative setting of Acts shifts from Judea to the Diaspora. But even then, Luke mentions this idol worship only rarely, and mildly. The so-called Apostolic Council in Jerusalem, sending a letter to gentile believers in Antioch, advises them "to abstain from what has been sacrificed to idols, and from blood and from what has been strangled, and from fornication" (Acts 15.29). Paul, traveling to Athens, is "deeply distressed to see that the city was full of idols" (17.16), and he urges the Athenians to repent before the day of judgment (17.16, 29–31). Finally, in Ephesus, an irate idol-maker complains to others in his guild about Paul's successes: "This Paul has persuaded and drawn away a considerable number of people by saying that gods made with hands are not gods" (19.26). The full-throated denunciation of pagan worship sounded so strongly in the genuine Pauline letters plays as a diminuendo in Acts.

Acts does denounce idol worship dramatically and vigorously, however. But the ethnic identity of the idolaters has changed. In Luke's telling, idolatry becomes the *Jewish* sin par excellence. Looking back, as did Paul, to the incident of the Golden Calf described in Exodus 32 (cf. 1 Corinthians 10), Luke mobilizes the story to serve not as a warning to pagans about the dangers of idol worship but as a description of an abiding proclivity of Jews. Luke sounds this new note in a passage of highest drama when Stephen, "full of grace and power," concludes his review of Israelite history before the hostile Sanhedrin in Jerusalem.

Israel has always been balky, Stephen observes, rejecting Moses after God sent him to rescue them from Egypt (Acts 7.35), turning their hearts back to Egypt rather than obeying him (7.39). "Instead, they pushed him aside,... saying to Aaron, 'Make gods for us who will lead the way for us.'... And they made a calf, offered a sacrifice to the idol, and reveled in the *works of their hand*" (7.39–41). God turned away from them, Stephen continues, and "handed them over to worship the host of heaven" (stars, planets, and the deities associated with them, 7.42); that is, Luke writes, leaping from the period in the wilderness to the period of the monarchy and of the First Temple, God handed Israel over to the worship of foreign gods:

> As it is written in the book of the prophets,
>
> "Did you offer to me slain victims and sacrifices, forty years in the wilderness, O house of Israel? No! You took along the tent of Moloch, and the star of your god Rephan, *the images that you made* to worship; so I will remove you beyond Babylon." (Acts 7.42–43; cf. Amos 5.25–27)

Stephen then criticizes the building of the temple itself , which is (or had been, by the time that Luke composes his story, c. 100) the place of Israel's sacrifices. "The Most High does not dwell in houses *made with human hands*," Stephen continues, quoting Isaiah 66.1–2: "Made by hand" and like phrases, which I have italicized above, code for the idols of foreign gods; but in Stephen's accusation, through Luke's tight juxtaposing, the phrase *also* codes for the temple. When has Israel *not* worshiped idols and false gods? When have they *not* dishonored God? This fundamental sin, the blatant violation of the very first commandment, was the whole reason why God had sent his prophets to Israel. But Israel used this summons to repentance as an opportunity to sin even more:

> You stiff-necked people, uncircumcised in heart and ears, you are forever opposing the holy spirit, *just as your ancestors used to do.* Which of the prophets did your ancestors not persecute? They killed those who foretold the coming of the Righteous One [Jesus], and now *you have become his betrayers and murderers.* You received the law . . . and yet you have not kept it. (Acts 7.51–53)

From the nation's very beginnings right up to the present day, says Stephen/Luke, Israel has never *not* been attracted to idols. The prophets came repeatedly to turn them from false worship, and repeatedly Israel rejected them, even killed them. But Luke here has cinched this accusation to another, more terrible one: it is the Jews who killed Jesus.[27]

In his lengthy *Dialogue with Trypho*, Justin repeats these accusations. Like Luke, he changes the "ethnicity" of idol worship. Demon worship, idolatry, and blood sacrifices—now paradigmatic *Jewish* sins—eventuate in Israel's murderous rejection of the prophets, of Christ, and of (Justin's) Christianity. These arguments serve a vital function, enabling Justin to read the Septuagint as a work of *exclusively* Christian revelation. (As he says to his Jewish interlocutor when reviewing Christological passages in psalms and prophets, "Are you familiar with these, Trypho? They are contained in your scriptures—or, rather, *not yours, but ours,*" *Trypho* 29.) If Christ were the go-between god so active in the Bible, then Christ was and always had been the proper object of *Jewish* worship. Indeed, the great spiritual heroes of Israel—Moses, David, Isaiah—had realized this, which was why their works, when read with true spiritual understanding (as Justin and his community read them), yield so many symbolic and prophetic references to their actual divine source, Christ himself (*Trypho* 29, and passim, esp. 127).

But most Jews throughout their generations had missed the fundamental meaning of their own law. Instead, ignorant of the law's true referent, they enacted revelation *kata sarka*, in a fleshly way, performing its spiritual tenets as physical acts: circumcision, purifications, Sabbath protocols, food laws, and most especially blood sacrifices. But true circumcision, corrects Justin, is not of the body but of the heart (*Trypho* 15–16, and frequently); true purification comes only through faith in the blood of Christ (*Trypho* 13), and so on. When Trypho finally protests that Justin selects and quotes "whatever you wish from the prophetic writings, but do not refer to those that expressly command" observance, Justin responds with a ringing indictment: "You [Jews] are a people hard-hearted and without understanding, both blind and lame, children in whom is no faith, as he himself says, honoring him only with your lips, far from him in your hearts, teaching doctrines that are your own and not his" (*Trypho* 27).

The Jews, claims Justin, are and always have been obdurate and spiritually blind. They expressed these intrinsic faults from their very birth as a nation, in the immediate aftermath of the redemption from Egypt, when they made and worshiped the Golden Calf (*Trypho* 19–23). The perduring Jewish addiction to idolatry and the Jews' proverbially stony hearts in turn explain the second great function of the law: not only to prophecy Christ, but also to discipline and punish fleshly Israel. Its myriad details about offerings were God's effort to distract Israel from idol worship. ("Your ungrateful nation . . . made a Calf in the wilderness, where God, accommodating himself to that nation, enjoined them also to offer sacrifices *as if* to his name, in order that you might not serve idols" *Trypho* 19; cf. 43.) So also with the temple: God did not need a house, but he permitted it "so that you would not worship idols" (*Trypho* 22). So also with the food laws (and the Calf again):

> You were commanded to abstain from certain kinds of food in order that you might keep God before your eyes while you ate and drank, since you were prone to depart from his knowledge, as Moses himself affirms: "The people ate and drank, and rose up to play." (Ex 32.6; *Trypho* 20)

But why then, Trypho challenges, long after the incident of the Golden Calf, did the prophets continue to proclaim as God's will the same commandments as he had given through Moses? For the very same reason, answers Justin: "On account of your hardness of heart and your ingratitude toward him . . . so that if you repent you might please him, and not *sacrifice your children to demons*, . . . nor fail to do judgment for orphans, nor justice to widows, nor have your hands full of blood" (*Trypho* 27, Justin's segue to Isaiah 1–2; for repeated accusations of such sacrifice, see 19; 73; 133). The question, really, is, when has Israel ever *not* worshiped idols?

Justin's presentation of Israel as always and everywhere prone to idolatry allows him to adapt and to mobilize yet another Jewish tradition, this one preserved in the pseudepigraphic *Lives of the Prophets*. These late Second Temple legends, amplifying the canonical prophets' complaints about resistance to their message, related lurid tales of the prophets' murders by their own recalcitrant people. Justin evokes them to develop a "trail of blood" motif: the Jews' obtuseness, and their perennial attachment to idol worship, led them first to kill the prophets, and then to kill the one whom they prophesied,— that is, Jesus. Not content with that, Justin goes on, the Jews continue right into the present to persecute Christians, cursing them in synagogues and spreading calumnies about them among the pagans, "so that you are the cause not only of your own unrighteousness, but in fact of that of all other men" (*Trypho* 16–17).

So blind are the Jews to the true meaning of scripture, so mindlessly attached to their own carnal interpretations of the law, that they did not repent of killing Jesus even after his resurrection; instead, they circulated rumors that his disciples had stolen his body. They accused Jesus of being the source of "godless, lawless, and unholy doctrines"—a reference to popular accusations of Christian cannibalism and sexual profligacy— and thereby incited pagan fury. And even still, Justin continues, the Jews persevere in their malice and their obduracy despite the crushing defeats inflicted on them by Rome. "Your city is captured and your land ravaged," he asserts (*Trypho* 108), alluding both to the Roman destruction of Jerusalem and the temple in 70, and to the more recent events of the Bar Kokhba revolt in 132–135, the temporal setting of the dialogue (*Trypho* 1). The facts of history, Justin urges, validate his argument. God had never desired blood sacrifices. He had inaugurated them solely because of Israel's abiding sinfulness in worshiping idols; he brought the law to a definitive end in Christ (*Trypho* 43). God has no more patience with the Jews' carnal interpretations of biblical revelation, and through Roman agency has made the carnal interpretation of the law impossible. Israel has nowhere left to offer sacrifices.

Yet prophetic revelation, Justin avers, also foretells that Jerusalem will not lie in ruins forever. Citing Isaiah and Ezekiel, Justin strongly affirms Trypho's statement that Jerusalem will be rebuilt, enlarged and adorned, and that the patriarchs, prophets, and proselytes will be gathered there together with many people to rejoice with the messiah (*Trypho* 80). There they will reign with Christ for a thousand years, after which time the general resurrection and final judgment will occur (*Trypho* 81; Revelation 20.4–5). Justin presents this idea in explicit contrast to Christian "blasphemers" who deny bodily resurrection and who hold that redemption concerns only the soul, and not also the physical body (*Trypho* 80). Flesh itself, Justin insists, will be redeemed.

This vision of redemption represents the nodal point where Justin's biblical interpretation and cosmology, his incarnational Christology, and his appropriation of Christianity's Jewish heritage all come together. By conceptualizing Christ both as the son of the high god *and* as that god's agent in framing the material cosmos (thus, as the deity active in the Septuagint), he domesticated the flesh for the Christian message. Flesh was not intrinsically alien to redemption; it was not the product of a disruption or accident in the upper heavens. Flesh was the good divinity's chosen medium. (Not that Justin's god created matter: rather, he worked with preexistent, unformed matter, hyle; 1 *Apology* 10, 59.) And if flesh were not alien to the biblical divinity and his father, then when they created humanity, they could create humanity enfleshed. In other words, while Justin no less than his theological competitors saw humans as tripartite in nature—spirit or mind/soul/fleshly body—he could assert that flesh was also an essential part of human being. Humans were not just their spirit or mind but also and no less their flesh.

And again, since the framer and shaper of flesh was the immediate agent of the high god, nothing impeded Christ from truly assuming flesh when he finally appeared in history: "Christ, who appeared for our sakes, became the whole rational being, body, reason, and soul" (2 *Apology* 10). "Jesus Christ . . . took both flesh and blood for our salvation" (1 *Apology* 66). But why? Because Adam and Eve's sin of disobedience had made human flesh mortal (*Trypho* 88). By dying and rising in the flesh, Christ conquered death, making flesh immortal (*Trypho* 63). Those saved in him would rise immortal at their own resurrection. And in the indefinite meantime, the Christian could be nourished and transformed by the Eucharist, "the flesh and blood of Jesus, who was made flesh" (1 *Apology* 66). Neither flesh nor matter, then, was something that the Christian had to escape in order to be saved.[28]

Both Valentinus and Marcion seem to have envisaged salvation as the individual's passage through the cosmos to a transcendent realm beyond, the realm of the high god. Justin's view of flesh, by contrast, impelled him to regard salvation as a communal and a historical event, to be accomplished in the last days (*Trypho* 80). In this respect his thought was both like and unlike Paul's, both like and unlike other Jewish apocalyptic thinking. The communal and historical dimension of redemption that Justin sketches in *Trypho* corresponds to Paul's instruction in 1 Thessalonians and in 1 Corinthians 15. Paul's tone of urgency, however, is utterly gone. Paul had expected these final events to unwind within his own lifetime. Justin, though he affirms an eschatological scenario, deals with a much broader time frame, several cycles of a thousand years (which, he admits, are "predicted obscurely," *Trypho* 81). Justin does not seem to anticipate the "final days" falling in his own.[29]

Paul had stated emphatically that the resurrection body would be *pneumatikon*, "spiritual," definitely not flesh and blood (1 Cor 15.44, 50). The raised meet Christ "in the clouds . . . in the air" (1 Thes 4.15). Justin's saints, by contrast, convene on earth—where else could flesh and blood go?—and reign in the restored Jerusalem. On this point, Justin stands closer to later rabbinic eschatology than Paul does. The terrestrial location of Christ's kingdom allows Justin to avail himself of the rich imagery of the prophets, such as Isaiah 65 ("There shall be a new heaven and a new earth . . . and I will rejoice over Jerusalem," *Trypho* 81). And such appropriation was another way to make his case that the Septuagint was a book of Christian revelation, and that the promises in scripture made to Israel about their final redemption—those promises that Paul referred to in Romans 15.3—would be realized not by the "old" Israel, *vetus Israel*, but by the "true" Israel, Justin's own community, the *verus Israel* of the church (*Trypho* 123).

Beleaguered by his Christian competition; challenged, perhaps, by skeptical Jews; eventually persecuted by incensed pagans: Justin is not much moved to define or to discuss the sins of his own community. Rather, he dwells at great length on the sins of others, defining his group as the sole innocent—and right-thinking—society. Heretics, victims of their own pride and faulty reasoning, blaspheme against God and secretly commit gross indecencies and murders. Pagans—perhaps the least culpable of these three groups of outsiders—are unwittingly led astray by the deceits of demons. Jews, the very worst of all, are innately bloody-minded, committed idolaters, repeat offenders in every generation.

The sins of all these others give us a reverse (and idealized) image of Justin's own community: sober, chaste, pious, self-disciplined—in short, genuinely philosophical. They alone, in effect, do *not* sin. Justin's Christ, in consequence, saves the true believer not from sin as such (correct belief has already done that) but from the pollution caused by sin (*Trypho* 13, with reference specifically to purity obtained through Christ's blood). And eschatologically, Christ will save those who believe in him from the universal consequence of sin: by coming in the flesh and by dying in the flesh, Christ had conquered and would conquer humanity's last enemy, death itself.

Chapter 3
A RIVALRY OF GENIUS

Sin and Its Consequences in Origen and Augustine

For Jesus of Nazareth as for his later followers, sin was an event or an activity that ruptured the relationship between a person and God. Jews were guided in their efforts to avoid sin and to please their god by his revelation on Sinai, and especially by the Ten Commandments. But the god of Israel evidently did not expect perfection, because his Torah also gave guidelines for the ways in which his people were to deal with sin. These included repentance, restitution where possible (especially if the victim of the sinner's wrongdoing were another person), atonement, and sacrifice.

Jesus, convinced that God's kingdom approached, called his hearers to prepare for that event specifically by renouncing their sins: "Repent, for the kingdom of God is at hand! Repent, and trust in the good news"—the good news that God was about to redeem his people (Mk 1.15). But redeem them from what? Not from sin as such (repentance effected a person's turning

Figure 4. Ravenna portrait of Paul. *Apostolus haereticorum,* Tertullian had called Paul, the "apostle of the heretics." Paul's letters, in the centuries after his death, proved amazingly interpretable, sustaining the theological perspectives of a wide range of mutually combative Christian communities. In the third and fourth centuries, even within the self-designated "orthodox" church, the interpretation of his letters, especially Romans, grew increasingly fractious. We see the broad lines of this interpretive battle in comparing the contrasting theologies of Origen of Alexandria (185–254) and of Augustine of Hippo (354–430). And in their work we see as well the endpoint of sin's transition from individual misdeed to universal condition. Photo courtesy Scala/Art Resource, New York. Archbishop's Palace, Ravenna, Italy.

from sin) but from sin's consequences: disease, death, dispersion. Indeed, from the perspective of apocalyptic prophecy, the establishment of God's kingdom represented, for Israel and for all peoples, a redemption from history.

Here the larger contemporary context of Jewish restoration theology, as we have seen, helps us to interpret these spare gospel traditions (see p. 13). Many of its themes can be found in the writings of the prophet Isaiah. At the End, foresees the prophet, the mountain of God's house will be raised above all the mountains: it will draw all peoples to the worship the god of Jacob (Is 2.2–4). Pagans will turn from their false gods, and Israel will return from the lands of their dispersion—from Assyria, from Egypt, from Ethiopia; indeed, from the four corners of the earth (11.11–16). A Davidic king will arise to rule over both the reassembled Israel and over the nations: "Him shall the nations seek" (11.10). At the End, God will make a feast for all peoples, who will converge at the temple, in his city, Jerusalem (25.6).

Jesus had restricted his mission to Israel. His message of this impending redemption penetrated the synagogues of the Diaspora only in the years that followed his death, and his disciples' experience of his resurrection. (Expectation of the resurrection of the dead was another prominent element in Jewish eschatology. His disciples' perception of Jesus as raised gives us the measure of their own apocalyptic convictions: Jesus' resurrection confirmed that the kingdom truly was at hand; 1 Cor 15.3–8, 12; cf. Acts 1.6.) Especially with its move into the Diaspora came gentile interest in the mission, and the mission's interest in the gentiles. So too, accordingly, came the emphasis that we see in Paul's letters on *gentile* sin: the worship of other gods, of the idols that represented them, and the indulgence in *porneia*, sexual transgression, which Jewish tradition saw as idolatry's invariable accompaniment.

In Paul's view, the entire universe stood under the power of sin—or, rather, of Sin. Nonetheless, empowered by spirit through baptism, Paul's pagans had turned from their sinful worship of these cosmic forces and dedicated themselves to the gospel. They lived according to the tenets of God's law and "wait[ed] for his Son from heaven" (1 Thes 1.10), whose return would mark the subjection of these powers and the universal acknowledgment of Israel's god (1 Cor 15.23–28). In the (foreshortened) present, Christ as eucharistic sacrifice replaced for these baptized pagans their former sacrifices to their own gods, and empowered them to turn from sin; in the near future, Christ as returning triumphant warrior would literally defeat "the last enemy, Death" (1 Cor 15.26). Saved humanity together with all creation would be "released from its bondage to decay" (Rm 8.21); the fleshly bodies both of the dead and of the living would be transformed into "spiritual bodies" (1 Cor 15.44). In the End, throughout the cosmos, God would reign supreme.

These Jewish apocalyptic ideas about sin and redemption, refracted through the prism of later second-century Greco-Roman learned culture, proved broadly interpretable. We have seen how Valentinus, Marcion, and Justin, three gentile Christian theologians from the earlier half of that century, arrived at their respective ideas of sin by interpreting the Christian message within the wider context of pagan *paideia*. In so doing, all three reinterpreted, and so diminished, the earliest movement's commitment to an imminent end of time. Allied as they were to non-Jewish forms of high culture, all three also altered the ethnic identity of God. The god of Jesus and of Paul had been, emphatically, the god of Abraham, Isaac, and Jacob; the god of Jewish history; the god of Israel. The high god of these gentile theologians, by contrast, was the nonethnic, non–historically active, radically transcendent deity of philosophy. The creator god of the Septuagint, on the other hand, retained for them his ethnic identification as the god of Israel. For Valentinus as for Marcion, this Jewish god had little to do with the redemption wrought through Christ. For Justin, this Jewish god *was* Christ, before his incarnation.

For all three theologians—as for Paul before them—"flesh" stood as rhetorical shorthand for "sin." For Justin, however, the sins of the flesh, and especially idolatry, were expressed most significantly not in pagan culture so much as in all non-Christian Jewish culture: for Justin, idol worship was the *Jewish* sin par excellence. Those blood sacrifices that Jesus and Paul would have viewed positively as a divinely mandated step in the process of atonement for sin Justin saw as a standing indictment of the Jews' abiding inclination toward idolatry. Both Jesus and Paul, in Justin's view, as well as the Hebrew prophets who had spoken of Christ, had all preached against sacrifices and against the temple cult. The only true sacrifice was that of Christ himself.

For all three thinkers, finally, Christ redeemed from death and, thus, from sin; but each imagined this redemption differently. The saved Valentinian or Marcionite Christian escaped the realm of sinful flesh at and through physical death, ascending as living spirit through the heavens to the realm of the high god and his Son. The redeemed Christian according to Justin, however, received flesh back again in a bodily resurrection, in a restored Jerusalem, at the end of time: when it came, the kingdom would arrive on earth.

With Origen of Alexandria (187–254), our third-century theologian, and with Augustine of Hippo (354–430), our late fourth-/early fifth-century thinker, this ancient Christian conversation about sin alters markedly. Unlike our second-century figures, who each turned to different bodies of sacred texts, both Origen and Augustine shared the same scriptural canon, Old Testament and New, which they saw as together articulating a single divine initiative of redemption. Both saw themselves as standing within and as speaking for the same "true church" of Christian orthodoxy. And they were similarly situated intellectually and polemically: Origen wrote with the competing theologies of Valentinus and Marcion in view; Augustine with the Manichees—a fourth-century avatar of these earlier communities—at his back and on his mind.

But what distinguished the work of these later theologians so definitively from that of their second-century counterparts was its scope and its richness, both qualitatively and quantitatively. Their respective readings of the Bible incorporated extraordinarily creative improvisations of the late Platonic tradition in which they both stood. And both men were prodigiously productive. Origen, according to Jerome, wrote over two thousand treatises, of which we know the titles of some eight hundred. He commented on every book in the Bible, the Old Testament text of which he sought to establish in a critical edition (the *Hexapla*). He wrote a definitive apology for Christianity against paganism (*Against Celsus*), and composed near numberless sermons and scholia (brief investigations of difficult passages). Finally, he conceived and crafted *On First Principles*, the church's very first systematic theology, which attempted to present a coherent interpretation of Christian doctrine. Augustine, no less productive, left behind a corpus of some five million words: commentaries, theological treatises, polemical tracts, sermons, letters—the equivalent, one recent biographer has calculated, of producing a modern 300-page book a year every year for almost forty years.[1]

Finally, both of these later theologians were acutely attuned to the problem of binding the representations of God in the Old Testament together with those in the New Testament. Their heretical competition forced the problem on them. Both, accordingly, turned to Paul as a major authority for the orthodox perspective—not least because Paul figured so prominently in the theologies of their competitors as the warrant for repudiating the Jewish scriptures and the Jewish god. To retrieve Paul from these other Christians, to offer a coherent reading of orthodoxy's double canon, and to account more globally for the problem of evil—if the creator god were a good god, then why is the world that he made so bad?—each placed the idea of sin at the very center of his theology. For Origen, sin explained even the organization of the physical cosmos: its ranks of stars and planets, its celestial and terrestrial powers, its earth-centered core, its population of embodied souls. For Augustine, sin accounted for the very processes of human consciousness, for every detail of human sexual intimacy, for the very structure of language, even of a single word.

Their shared focus on Paul and their mutual adherence to the principles of late Platonism notwithstanding, however, these two geniuses of the ancient church also disagreed sharply. According to Origen, Paul's message was that all will be saved; according to Augustine, Paul's message was that all should be damned. According to Origen, all rational beings by definition have free will; according to Augustine, humanity left to its own devices can only sin. According to both Origen and Augustine, God's two great moral attributes are justice and mercy. But Origen's god expresses these attributes universally and simultaneously: God is *both* just *and* merciful. Augustine's god expresses these attributes serially and selectively: he is *either* just *or* merciful. For Origen, even Satan will at last attain redemption; for

Augustine, even infants, if unbaptized, go to hell. And their ultimate fates as doctors of the church differed no less sharply than did their signature theological views. Augustine the late Latin bishop and renowned controversialist became a saint, and one of the premier authorities of western Christendom. Origen, lay intellectual and Christian martyr, was ultimately condemned as a heretic, his great literary legacy destroyed.

How did these two theologians, despite all of their common commitments, come to such differing estimations of the nature and consequences of sin? For our answer we will begin with Origen, and with the vast vision that he lays out in his shattered masterpiece, *On First Principles*.[2]

On First Principles is a systematic theology, an effort to understand in a coherent and coordinated way the full scope of God's relation to the universe from its creation outside of time to its final redemption. To present his vision, Origen expounds in four books his understanding of God (book I), of the material universe (book II), of rational being (thus free will; book III), and of revelation (that is, scripture; book IV).

Before embarking on his exposition, Origen lays out his doctrinal presuppositions in a creedal-sounding preface. These align him securely with the self-designated "orthodoxy" of his third-century church. "All who believe and are convinced that grace and truth came by Jesus Christ and that Christ is the Truth," he begins, "derive [this] knowledge from no other source but the very words and teaching of Christ." This teaching, he continues, is to be found both in the New Testament (from the period "when [Christ] was made man and dwelt in the flesh") and in the Old ("since even before that [time], Christ the Word of God was in Moses and the prophets," *On First Principles* I.

praef., 1). Noting that many Christians who hold this belief nonetheless have conflicting opinions about important issues, Origen also invokes ecclesiastical tradition, "the teaching of the church handed down in unbroken succession from the apostles." Canonical scripture and apostolic teaching together are the guarantors of correct doctrine (I. praef., 2).

But apostolic doctrine, like scripture itself, Origen notes, has many different levels. Its plainest meanings even the dull-minded grasp. God's book holds deeper or higher meanings, however, and these beckon to those readers who, loving wisdom, train themselves through intellectual exercise to become worthy and capable of receiving them (I. praef., 3). Presenting a crisp punch list of doctrinal fixed points—God is one; the Son and the Spirit are also God; the Son was incarnate in human flesh; human will is free; the devil and his angels oppose the good, and so on—Origen notes as well a sweep of issues on which the church "does not speak clearly" (I. praef., 4–10). These obscurities invite diligent believers to sound scripture's depths, aided by the disciplined application of allegorical or "spiritual" interpretation.[3]

What, then, of the nature of God? Origen begins his exploration with a concept lightly touched on in his preface, the notion of bodilessness. The Bible (and most believers, he notes) do not know the term *incorporeal* (*asomaton*; I. praef., 8), but that idea is key to understanding God. Sometimes, indeed, scripture speaks of God as if he had or was a body, though he does not. (Even words like *light* or *fire* suggest this; subtle body, however, is body nonetheless; *On First Principles* I. i, 1.) But God is beyond all body, Origen asserts: God is *purely* spirit, utterly invisible, absolutely without any extension in space (I. i, 6; II. ii, 2). This supreme deity Origen identifies as Trinity: Father, Son, and Holy Spirit. These relate to each other in ways that leave room for speculation—how can the Son be the image of God? How can something invisible be said to have an "image" (I. ii, passim)? Does the Holy Spirit relate to God like the Son does, or in some other way (I. praef., 4)?—but this "threeness," Origen asserts, does not compromise God's radical simplicity, his oneness (I. i, 6; I. iii., 41). Like the Father, the Son and the Holy Spirit are also absolutely without body. They/he alone are intrinsically good by nature ("essentially good," I. v, 3). They/he are absolutely unique.

Against the theologies of Valentinus and Marcion, Origen insists that God the Father is the god of Israel: he is the Creator (though with a difference, as we shall see), the single source of the law, the prophets and the gospel (1. praef., 4). Yet this deity also exhibits the characteristics of the high god of philosophical paideia. He is self-existing: everything else that is is contingent upon him. He is radically perfect, which means that he alone is completely changeless. And, again, he is absolutely without body of any sort; *only* God is *asomaton*. Logically, these principles have immediate implications for God's creation. Everything that is not God has body of some sort, because only God is without body. Everything that is not God is contingent, dependent upon God for its own existence, because only God is self-existing. Everything that is not God is, ipso facto, subject to change, because only God is absolutely and perfectly without change. Hold fast these last three ideas: they will account for Origen's concept of sin.

What, then, is not God? To phrase the same question differently: given God's radical changelessness, what and how does he "create"? Origen answers ingeniously with his doctrine of double creation. The first "creation," he explains, was eternal. That is, before time existed—which is to say, before matter existed—God (always) presided over a universe of eternally generated (that is, timelessly generated) rational beings. Origen grants that this is not an easy concept. ("In this matter human intelligence is feeble and limited, when it tries to understand how during the whole of God's existence his creatures have existed also . . . without a beginning," I. iv, 4. Later Christian theologians will appeal to the same idea to explain how the Son is eternally generated by the Father.) An eternally generated creation protects God against any imputation of change.[4]

This nonmaterial creation was a population of rational beings, since they were eternally generated according to the image of God's Image, his Logos or rationality. Since not God, these individual beings *did* have bodies, but these bodies were immaterial and, obviously, eternal—or, as Paul says in 1 Corinthians 15.44, "spiritual." *Body* here serves as a principle of individuation. In the eternal realm, nonmaterial or spiritual body distinguished one rational being from another (*On First Principles* II. ii, 2)—an important consideration, since each individual being is judged on its own merit. And these individual creatures qua rational beings had an absolutely unimpeded capacity to choose between good and evil. Put differently—in the idiom of Greek moral philosophy rather than in the hybrid biblical idiom of Origen's theology—free will is constitutive of all rational being.[5]

For Origen as for the tradition of philosophy that he drew upon, however, "free will" was not a neutral capacity to choose between good and evil. In this metaphysical system, the soul or its *nous*, the ensouled mind, has a kind of natural kinship with the One, which itself is also absolute truth and good. ("Men have a kind of blood-relationship with God," Origen claims, which accounts for the progress in spiritual understanding that the mind can make; IV. iv, 9).When the mind apprehends truth, it loves truth: "knowing" implies "loving." (Plato, of course, is the prime source for this idea of the erotic quality of knowledge.) *Hamartia*, "sin"—a turning from God—accordingly implies *error*, since no one would ever knowingly turn from truth or willingly make a mistake. Ignorance impedes right choices; knowledge occasions and sustains them. In brief, "sin" as moral error has an inescapably intellectual dimension: one chooses according to what one knows. Once one knows the truth, one turns freely to the truth, because one loves it.

What, then, according to Origen, is the origin of sin? How and why do these rational beings, with their full power of free choice, even come to sin? And what is sin? His god's uniqueness and changelessness imply the answer. Since only God is, by nature, changeless, his creatures, as not God, have an innate tendency to change. *Since it is innate, this tendency to change is not culpable.* (God would be unjust to punish his creature for something that it could not help but do.) But in the world before time and matter, this innate tendency had cosmic consequences.

To explain the primordial transition from an eternal, spiritual creation to the world of matter, change, and time, Origen speculates that these primordial souls, or their love, "cooled." (The idea invokes the old Platonic wordplay of *psuchē*, "soul," and *psuchesthai*, "to cool"; *On First Principles* II. vii, 3.) In the time before time, these beings became distracted, in effect turning "from" God. "Turning from God," in philosophical theology, codes for *sin. Again, since this ancient slippage was "natural," it was not culpable.* God could not with justice punish his creatures for *not* being unchanging or for *not* being perfect, as he himself is. ("Essential goodness," as Origen notes, "is found solely in Christ and in the Holy Spirit, and of course in the Father also," I. v, 3.) By virtue of these souls' being contingent, thus "created," they were *eo ipso* changeable.

What *was* culpable, however, was that these souls initially failed to move their will in order to brake their decline from God. Different rational beings—which, since God is just, all had identical moral capacity—only stopped their decline eventually, and at various "distances" from God. Their variety of stopping points, in effect, mark off a precosmic fall of the soul, the first sin. More than just humanity erred in this way: "humans," for Origen, does not exhaust the category "rational beings." The plenum of angelic and supernatural powers (including Satan and all those who currently oppose God, I. v, 1–5), as well as the sun, moon and stars (which are also rational intelligences, I. vii, 1–4): all but one member of this radically egalitarian spiritual fellowship turned, slipped, stopped only eventually, and therefore sinned. The great and sole exception was the rational being who freely chose to love God absolutely. That soul so loved God that it "fused with the divine Logos" (II. vi, 3): it would enter history as Jesus. All the rest stopped at different points, depending on their individual exercise of will.[6]

In the face of the Fall, then, God in his justice and mercy "acted" to effect his creatures' redemption. Out of absolutely nothing, he called matter into being (II. i, 1–4).[7]

"Now since the [present] world is so very varied and comprises so great a diversity of rational beings," observes Origen, "what else can we assign to the cause of its existence except the diversity in the fall of those who declined from unity in dissimilar ways?" (II. i, 1). This diversity of circumstances, articulated in the diversity of material bodies in the universe, expresses the diversity of moral responses that these rational beings made to their decline from God and the good. God in his mercy and justice, in other words, arranged the wonderfully plastic medium of matter, or "flesh," to accommodate all these different ethical levels of accomplishment or failure. To what end? So that the individual soul, embodied in its precise historical/material circumstances, can learn through those circumstances how it erred, can consequently repent of its particular failings, and can freely turn in love back to God.

Thus, like the Valentinians and Marcionites against whom he argues, Origen also saw the fleshly body as a secondary, nonessential part of the self. For him as for them, the fleshly body measured the fall of the soul. And for him as for them, the fleshly body represented what the soul, when redeemed, had to leave. But *unlike* these other Christians, Origen saw flesh *qua* flesh as "good," the gracious and providential gift of the good god, created as an aid to salvation. The entire material universe, Origen taught, is a school for souls; the material body, a temporary and propaedeutic device. All the different kinds of bodies that exist in this secondary world (including celestial bodies, I. vii, 4) register the moral trajectory of their souls' previous freely willed decisions. God places the soul of each fallen rational being into precisely the sort of material circumstance that it needs in order to learn what it needs to know in order to return to God.

God is patient and infinitely resourceful; his providence micromanages the material universe; he has all the time in the world. (And since rational beings are also eternal, so do they.) Once every last rational being has finally learned what it needs to learn in order to freely choose to love God, matter will sink back into the nothing whence it came. Ethnicity, gender, social station: all the contingencies of historical existence drop away. The "saints" will rise in their "spiritual bodies" (III. vi, 5–9). Even Satan and his minions will at last come around (I. vi, 3; III. v, 5–6), because God loves all his creatures, and he wants all to be saved. Thus, since "the end is always like the beginning" (I. vi, 2), these spiritually embodied rational beings in their totality, chastened by their long sojourn in history, will once again finally surround the incorporeal Godhead in love.[8]

To prove the reasonableness of all these propositions—that the soul has a long history of ethical choices before it appears in a historical, fleshly body; that God loves and providentially cares for all his creatures; that if God is just (and he is), then the choice of the will must be free (or else God would be unjust, whether in punishing or in rewarding)—Origen, in book III, turns particularly to Paul: "Let us see how Paul reasons with us as being men of free will and ourselves responsible for our destruction or salvation," (III. i, 6). Origen concentrates his remarks on Romans 9. There Paul had referred to three passages in the Old Testament notoriously hard to reconcile with a strong idea of moral freedom: the choice of Jacob over Esau "before either had been born" (Genesis 25.21–23), the hardening of Pharaoh's heart (Exodus 19), and God's forming persons as a potter forms clay pots, some as vessels of honor and some as vessels of dishonor (Isaiah 29.16, 45.9, 64.8; Jeremiah 18.6; cf. Romans 9.10–24). "These passages," Origen observes, "are in themselves sufficient to disturb ordinary people with the thought that man is not a free agent, but that it is God who saves and who destroys whomever he will" (III. i, 7).[9]

First, to Pharaoh: obviously he did not sin by nature, Origen observes, because then God would not have needed to harden his heart to ensure his disobedience. God's hardening Pharaoh proves just the opposite, that it was within Pharaoh's power to choose to obey. So why does a good and just God intervene in Pharaoh's moral decision by "hardening" him (III. i, 9–10)? The phrase, explains Origen, is a scriptural façon de parler. Just as a kind master will say to his servant who has been spoiled through the master's forbearance, "It was I who made you wicked," or "I am to blame for these offenses," so the Bible speaks of Pharaoh's heart being hardened: at the "fleshly" level of the text, the Exodus story presents God's forbearance as a kind of complicity in Pharaoh's sin. But in reality—seen, that is, from the perspective of eternity—God "allows" Pharaoh his freedom because Pharaoh *is* free. And God, master of providence, also knows that by Pharaoh's obstinacy other souls become obedient (like those of the Egyptians who chose to leave Egypt with Moses). Finally, God also knows that, through plagues and the drowning in the sea, "he is leading even Pharaoh" (III. i, 14).

But God's work with Pharaoh extends well beyond the borders of the Exodus story. "God deals with souls not in view of the fifty years of our life here," writes Origen, "but in view of the endless world. He has made our intellectual nature immortal and akin to himself, and the rational soul is not shut out from healing, as if this life were all" (III. i, 13). Behind these individual biblical episodes, as behind this mortal life itself, stands the endless shining plain of Origen's spiritual cosmos. And framing these stand Origen's ethics (if we want to look at this philosophically) or, rather, his commitment to a particular construction of the god of the Bible (if we want to look at this theologically). That god is both just and merciful. The image of the potter, from the prophets via Paul in Romans, in fact articulates the principle of God's scrupulous fairness. "Every soul in God's hands," urges Origen, "is of one nature, and all rational beings come, if I may say so, from one lump"—the *phurama* (Greek) or *massa* (Latin) of God's clay in Romans 9.21 (III. i, 22). No one, accordingly, is bad because he cannot be good: everyone, from Satan to Christ, was "created" equally, with exactly the same capacity for good or evil. The sole factor distinguishing all these rational beings one from another is their own individual exercise of will.

Origen's cosmology, accordingly, nullifies any problem of evil. In the light of eternity, there is no evil, only various temporal learning situations. Thus any difficulty with Jacob and Esau disappears: "The reasons why Jacob was loved and Esau hated," he explains, "lie with Jacob before he came into the body and with Esau before he entered Rebecca's womb" (III. i, 22; "hate," of course, is more scriptural façon de parler: God hates none of his creatures). The eternal souls of people, stars, demons—remember, humans do not exhaust the category of intelligent life—all make themselves, through their uncoerced choices, into vessels of honor or dishonor. But God is the impartial lover of souls, swaying considerate scales: he loves all his creatures equally, and works for all of them equally. The eternal damnation of any of his creatures would represent a failure on God's part. But God cannot fail. He throws no one away. He arranges matter, thus history, to facilitate his purpose of ultimate redemption.[10]

God works redemption through the Son, his Logos, the mediator between himself and creation, between himself and history. The Word's entry into human time with the incarnation effected a discrete moment, a turning point in the story of universal salvation. The incidents in Jesus' life on earth conformed to the ancient prophecies, thus revealing to the nations the divine authority of the Jewish scriptures. In consequence, these scriptures "have prevailed over the elect taken from among the nations. . . . For before the advent of Christ, it was not at all possible to bring forward clear proofs of the divine inspiration of the old scriptures. But the advent of Jesus led . . . to the clear conviction that they were composed with the aid of heavenly grace" (IV. i, 6). Christ through his incarnation revealed scripture itself as a medium of divine redemption, the charter of the church.

But if the Bible, with Jesus' advent, has been so clearly revealed to be God's word, why then do so many fail to interpret it correctly? Why is the (true) church not universally acknowledged? The Jews reject Christian claims because the prophecies of the messianic age went unfulfilled. (In Jesus' lifetime, Origen readily concedes, no leopards lay down next to lambs, no lions ate straw like oxen; IV. ii, 1.) The biblical text is full of references to God as labile or angry or jealous: he changes his mind about Saul (1 Sam 15.11), he "makes peace and creates evil" (Isa 45.7), he sends evils upon Jerusalem (Mic 1.12), and there are "ten thousand other passages like these." As a result, some readers think that the text refers only to the god of the Jews, the Creator, and "since the Creator [in their reading] is imperfect and not good, they think that the Savior came here to proclaim a more perfect god who they say is not the Creator, and about whom they entertain diverse opinions" (IV. ii, 1; Origen has Valentinians and Marcionites in mind). Finally, the "simple" believers within Origen's own church, while rightly thinking "that there is none greater than the Creator . . . believe such things of him as would not be believed of the most savage and unjust of men" (IV. ii, 1).

"Now the reason why all those whom we have mentioned hold false opinions or make impious or ignorant assertions about God appears to be nothing else but this," Origen explains, "that scripture is not understood in its spiritual sense, but is interpreted according to the bare letter" (IV. i, 2). Like all created being, and like the incarnate Christ himself, scripture, too, is tripartite, its levels of meaning corresponding to body or flesh (literal or historical meaning), soul (moral meaning), and spirit (its most profound and mystical meaning; IV. ii, 4). Mistakes accrue when one reads in only one way, or when one misreads a passage that should be read in another way. And even a spiritual reading will be incorrect unless it is guided by the apostolic teachings of Origen's church.

Origen does not discount or dismiss "bodily" meaning. After all, it was at this most empirical, this-worldly level that Christ became truly incarnate, and his church became known to the nations (IV. i, 6). The Bible is a book of history, containing "a record dealing with the visible creation, the formation of man and successive descendants, . . . stories of wars and conquerors" (IV. ii, 8). It holds many more passages that are both historically true *and* spiritually revelatory than ones "with purely spiritual meanings" (IV. iii, 4; passages of purely spiritual meaning do exist, however, IV. iii, 5). The "soulish" level of understanding is also very valuable, communicating important ethical teachings. (Origen points particularly to Exodus 20, the Ten Commandments, "useful quite apart from any spiritual interpretation," IV. iii, 4.) But only the spiritual meaning unveils the mystery of salvation, only spirit can reveal that "Israel is a race of souls, and Jerusalem a city in heaven" (IV. iii, 8).[11]

Origen's perspective from eternity cannot but foreshorten elements of earlier Christian tradition. Christ redeems from sin, but he does so not primarily by his incarnation as such nor by his death and bodily (though not fleshly) resurrection. "Sacrifice" as such is not the mechanism of, or prime metaphor for, salvation. Rather, Christ "saves" through his pedagogical function. He serves as a the ultimate example to believers of what soul absolutely untarnished by evil can accomplish in terms of intimacy with God (IV. iv, 4). "Death," in Origen's reckoning, also takes on metaphorical meaning, since the sinners who are now "subjected to death" are in essence immortal. So too "eternal fire" as sin's punishment: this is actually the sinful soul's *self*-torment, its own accusing conscience (II. x, 4). The "outer darkness" where sinners gnash their teeth is actually the darkness of deep ignorance (Mt 18.10; *On First Principles* II. x, 3). Scripture's punitive language masks the self-reflexive quality of these torments. God himself, the perfect and loving teacher, disciplines; he does not "punish."

The most profound meanings of all these events and states are metaphorical, pointing away from this time-bound world to the eternal one. This is so because time and the universe, Origen is convinced, are only passing players in the divine comedy. All rational beings, increasing in mind and intelligence, will eventually "advance to perfect knowledge," gazing "face to face" on the ultimate cause of all things, attaining perfection (II. xi, 7). In this sense, then, at the End, for all of his rational creation, God will be "all in all" (1 Cor 15.28).

Origen died in Caesarea in 254, a belated victim of the Decian persecution. His language was Greek, his philosophical education superlative. He was comfortable with interpretive ambiguities, frequently proffering multiple opinions and inviting his hearers to choose whichever one struck them as more reasonable (e.g., III. vi, 9). He was also a charismatic lifelong celibate. (Indeed, so untroubled was his asceticism that two rumors arose to account for it, one that Origen's serenity was achieved by drugs, the other, by the knife.) His circumstances and his temperament, in short, could not have been more different from Augustine's.[12]

Born in North Africa in 354, well after Constantine had thrown the empire's fortunes in with those of the church, Augustine had been a married man, the father of a son, and for more than ten years a Manichaean heretic. His secular career as a teacher of rhetoric ceded only eventually to his ecclesiastical one: baptized into the catholic church in 386, he became bishop of Hippo in 396. As a bishop, Augustine had political and institutional incentives to be clearer about doctrine—and certainly less speculative—than Origen had ever had to be: by Augustine's day, doctrine translated into public policy, bishops were a species of Roman magistrate, and imperial agents clarified theological disputes by force. His first-order awareness of the sexual, social, and political dimensions of human life profoundly affected the ways that Augustine understands sin. He explored these most especially in his huge masterwork, *City of God.*[13]

Augustine, further, had never really learned Greek, a limitation of incalculable consequence. He read both testaments of his Bible only in (clumsy) Latin translation, a fact that colors his views on language and interpretation as indices of sin's effects on the mind and the soul. And his knowledge both of pagan Greek philosophy and of the rich tradition of Greek patristic commentary, Origen's included, was limited to what he could get in Latin translation. This linguistic-intellectual isolation in one sense handicapped him; but it also compelled and even amplified his own fierce creativity. We see this most clearly in his idiosyncratic masterpiece, the *Confessions.*[14]

Finally, Augustine came of age theologically in the late 390s/ early 400s, just as the storm of the Origenist controversy burst upon—and blew apart—the pan-Mediterranean community of orthodox theologians. Theories of the soul's preexistence seemed suddenly uncomfortably close to heresy: Western tradition increasingly leaned toward seeing soul and body as beginning life together at the same time. And as souls became ever more incarnate, so too did history: the meaningful arena of God's activity shifted to events in this world. The faithful recited creeds asserting their belief in bodily, even fleshly resurrection. Hell's eternal fires burned too attractively to be renounced. And nobody wanted Satan to be saved.[15]

Different man, different temperament, different times—and very different views, consequently, on divine justice and mercy, and on the meaning and consequences of sin. These were the premier issues framing Augustine's life's work, from his commentaries on Paul's letter to the Romans against the Manichees in the 390s to his polemics against Pelagius and especially against Julian of Eclanum in the 420s. The historical and therefore the social dimension of sin; the linguistic and therefore the cognitive dimension of sin; God's justice and mercy toward sinners, and therefore the theological dimension of sin: these three components of his idea of sin all crystallized for Augustine around the figure of the first human being, Adam.

By the fourth century, Adam had had a long career in philosophical commentary on Genesis, for which he served as a symbol for the concept "mind." The roots of this allegory go back to first-century Hellenistic Jewish thought, to Philo of Alexandria's *On the Creation of the World*. In that work, Philo had decoded the story of the sin in the garden "spiritually," as a standing cautionary tale: when the senses ("Eve") are turned toward earthly things ("the serpent"), they can distract even the mind ("Adam"; *On the Creation of the World* 2.8; Augustine himself repeated this allegory some three centuries later, in his *Genesis against the Manichees*, 1.19, 30).

Besides relieving the reader of the story's literal embarrassments (Why is God so angry? Why does he not want Adam to know the difference between good and evil? Where did the snake come from?), such moralizing allegory much more readily accommodated a prime teaching of Platonism: Souls are by nature immortal, and accordingly their existence precedes life in the fleshly body. Contingent upon the divine, souls are none-theless like the divine in that they have no temporal beginning. Genesis, allegorically understood, was about the way that soul behaves, not the way that soul "begins."

Augustine's perspective came to shift from seeing Adam as an allegorical topos to seeing Adam as a concrete, historical personality. Within his theology, Adam begins to function as the individual ancestor of humanity, a person created body and soul together. Accordingly, Adam becomes as well the discrete point of origin for human sin and, thus, for human mortality. But these new considerations immediately complicate the idea of divine justice. How can God be just in punishing every generation of humanity for the sin of a single, distant ancestor?[16]

Origen had defended God's justice in visiting the conse-quences of sin on all rational beings by positing a corporate idea. Souls had no single ancestor; they all existed individually from eternity; all souls, except that of Jesus, sinned. Since all sinned, God was just in putting all into material bodies (though of various sorts, since different souls fell differently; see pp. 105ff.). And embodiment in any case was disciplinary, not penal. Augustine defends God's justice by positing a new and different corporate idea, that of "human nature." Adam indeed sinned as a discrete individual; but as the prime ancestor of the entire race, Adam had all humanity in some special way "in" him. His sin was "our" sin and "we" sinned when he sinned because in him *natura nostra peccavit*, "our nature sinned." In this way, according to Augustine, God's justice—punitive, not propaedeutic—fell on all humans equally.[17]

That punishment affected both body and soul. As a result of Adam's fall, the human body was made mortal, subject to death. ("We are born of earth, and we shall all go into the earth on ac-count of the first sin of the first man," Augustine says to a Manichaean opponent; *Against Fortunatus* 20.) But the soul, too, was affected, made "carnal"; all souls became oriented toward and susceptible to the importunings of sinful flesh. Sin, in this situation, easily became habit-forming; habit leads to compulsive behavior; such behavior by definition escapes control. Human will after the Fall, compromised in this way, in effect is not as free as it was in Adam before Adam sinned. Now a person can *want* not to sin: created by the good God, a person naturally desires the good. ("You have made us for yourself," writes Augustine, addressing God in the opening chapter of the *Confessions*, "and our hearts are restless until they rest in you," 1.1,1.) But after Adam, the will is defective: a person now functions with a sort of diminished capacity, unable if unassisted by grace to achieve the good.

God is still just in holding the sinner culpably responsible, however, even if the sinner cannot help but sin, for two reasons. First, the sinner (since he was "in Adam") suffers the universal penalty of Adam's sin—the will's diminished capacity—*justly*. And, second, though he cannot help but sin, he nonetheless sins freely in the sense that nothing *outside* of himself compels him to sin. A person sins because he *chooses* to sin. Since his sin is his own choice, he is punished justly.[18]

In his *Confessions*, Augustine brilliantly explored these ideas on sin and its consequences in part through the device of autobiographical narrative. In books 1 through 8 he provides a story about his own past, of his search for happiness (and, thus, for God, the only true source of happiness) in all the wrong places: in academic success, in social acceptance, in sex, in Manichaeism, in professional advancement. The story of his search peaks in book 8, where he provides an unforgettable portrait of his own indecision and divided will. In the end he converts, but only, he says, with the help of heaven.[19]

Augustine's life story ends with his baptism in book 9; but the *Confessions* goes on. Fully 40 percent of the work's eighty thousand words still remain, philosophically rich discussions of memory (book 10), time (book 11), language, scriptural interpretation, divine revelation (books 12 and 13). What emerges clearly from the soaring speculations of these difficult final books is the question that had driven Augustine's tale from its beginning: *How* can fallen humankind know God?

Why is finding God so difficult? After all, Augustine notes, God has provided many ways to know him: physical creation, which is his handiwork; his scriptures and his church; his divine Son, "who is the mediator between You the One and us the many" (11.29.39, with deliberate reference to the Platonic contrast). And the soul itself naturally longs for God (*Confessions* 1.1,1, quoted on p. 116). Especially via the higher part of the soul, the mind made according to the divine image and likeness, God has provided the royal road back to himself (Gen 1.26–27; *Confessions* 13.34,49). By turning inward, Augustine urges, a person can find God, who is "deeper in me than I am in me" (3.6,11).

But it is precisely here, in the deep self of the seeker, that sin has wrought its worst damage. Sin has ruptured the human self by tearing apart will and affect, thought and feeling. (For Augustine as for Origen, as for the Platonic tradition generally, knowing, willing, and loving are all functions of a unified mind.) As now constituted, a person cannot choose what she loves; and if she loves, she cannot will herself not to love. Love, the motor of the will, escapes the mind's control. After the Fall, every person's loves—good intentions notwithstanding—are misdirected *carnaliter*, and people act accordingly. What moves a person is not what she knows, but what she wants.

Augustine sums up this condition as the divided will: the mind knows one thing but wants something else; it thinks one thing but feels something else. Augustine sees Paul as describing this condition, the universal punishment for Adam's sin, in his letter to the Romans: "I do not understand my own actions. . . . I do not do what I want, but I do the very thing that I hate. . . . I can will what is right, but I cannot do it. I do not do the good that I want, but the evil that I do not want is what I do" (7.15–20). And Augustine memorably captures this paralyzing paradox of wanting and not wanting the same thing at the same time, describing his own struggle to commit to celibacy as his path into the catholic church, when he prayed *da mihi castitatem et continentiam, sed noli modo,* "Grant me chastity and continence; but not yet" (*Confessions* 8.7,17).

Even if the seeker's ruptured self wants to know God, it is confounded by another difficulty. A person's ability to know anything at all has been complicated and compromised by humanity's exile in time. After Eden, Augustine explains, the experience of time marks off crucial differences between the human mind—that is, God's image in humankind—and God himself. God is outside of time. He knows everything perfectly and (an aspect of this quality of knowing) he knows everything all at once, in "the simultaneity of eternity" (13.7,9). No gap whatsoever distinguishes divine knowing from divine willing and divine doing. Fallen humanity, however, has an utterly different experience of self and time. People know incompletely, they will ineffectively, they do imperfectly. Human consciousness is dislocated, distended by living in time.

Augustine cannot say what time is, but he gives a dizzying description of *how* time is (11.14,17). Time, he says, functions psychologically: its effects tell within the soul: "It is in you, my mind, that I measure time," 11.27,36). Time is measured by its flow, its ceaseless movement from the future (one type of nonbeing, since it does not yet exist) into the past (another type of nonbeing, since it no longer exists). The future is not yet; the past is no longer. Between these two plains of nonbeing that stretch out infinitely in either direction stands the singular reality of the present. Only the present actually *is*.

Yet the present itself is inherently ungraspable:

> If we can think of some bit of time that cannot be divided into even the smallest instantaneous moment, that alone is what we call "present." And this time flies by so quickly from the future into the past that it is an interval of no duration. . . . A present moment takes up no time. (11.15,20).

All of a person's consciousness, her ability to know and to understand, is circumscribed by and limited to this infinitely tiny, perpetually transient moment. Experience—by definition, solely in the present—ceaselessly runs between the fingers of the soul like sand. From this constant flow of atomized instances, how can a person possibly know anything, grasp anything?

To answer this question, Augustine thinks about language. Language, like thought, like experience, like consciousness, is also intrinsically distended in time. It too depends upon flow, a linear passage from being (present) to nonbeing (past). Consonants and vowels alternate to form phonemes, words follow words, nouns follow verbs. Both in its smallest units (consonants and vowels) and in its larger ones (words, sentences, and more), language works by having a beginning, a middle, and an end. (Augustine the ancient rhetorician thinks in terms of language spoken and heard, 11.6,8–11.11,3.) Only through the integrative functioning of memory can meaning be wrung from language. Once the end of a sound, a word, a sentence is reached, memory recalls the whole, and then interprets what the sounds convey.

Interpretation and understanding, the attainment of meaning, are thus the accomplishments of memory, whether for language or more broadly for experience itself. Meaning, in consequence, is never immediately present. It is always and necessarily mediated, retrospective, imperfect. This tenuousness of meaning—thus, of knowing—is symptomatic, claims Augustine, of humankind's penal situation in time. Truth without shadows, meaning without mediation, love without conflict, will come only at history's end, when time itself is swallowed up in "the Sabbath of eternal life" (13.36,51).

In *City of God*, painting across a huge canvas—twenty-two books, written in a period of over fifteen years, covering all of human history—Augustine further developed these ideas. Seen from one perspective, *City of God* is a universal history of the conflict between two sorts of love, *amor dei* (love of God) and *amor sui* (love of self), from the fall of Satan to the final redemption. Seen from another, *City of God* is a review of sin and of its terrible consequences for humanity, past (beginning in Eden), present (in the power relations of people, communities, societies, and empires), and future (when saints are saved and sinners finally and forever damned).

When God created humanity in the garden, Augustine asserts, he created him male and female, with bodies of flesh joined *ab initio* to spirit or soul. From this seemingly simple reading of Genesis Augustine draws some radical conclusions. First, and in sharp contrast to Origen, Augustine insists that God's choice to make body and soul together mean that *the fleshy body was the divinely willed habitat of the soul even before the Fall*. Second—even more radically, given the premium that contemporary Christianity placed on virginity and on sexual celibacy—Augustine insists that God's creation of Adam *and Eve* means that *even before the Fall* he had intended *humans to* be sexually active, *"to be fruitful and multiply" precisely through the sexual union of male and female.* Why else would God have bothered with gender?[20]

Augustine speculates on what sex without sin—thus, without the disorders of lust and without the humiliations of pleasure—would have been like. "The sexual organs would have been brought into activity by the same bidding of will as controlled the other organs. Then, without feeling the allurement of passion goading him on, the husband would have relaxed on his wife's bosom in tranquility of mind," without the "morbid condition" of lust, symbolized in and actualized by involuntary erection. Erection, ejaculation, insemination, conception: all would have occurred at will. Nor would sexual union have compromised virginity: "The male seed could have been dispatched into the womb with no loss of his wife's integrity, just as menstrual flux can now be produced from the womb of a virgin without loss of maidenhead" (*City of God* 14.26). Rational mind would have presided over sexual union. Body would have been under the complete control of the soul, which would have been in complete control of itself—the way that God had originally made Adam, the way that humanity had been supposed to be.

What had happened? Even though Adam had had complete freedom of will, being fully able not to sin, he chose instead to disobey the divine commandment. God thus struck him in the offending agent, the will itself; and since soul and body are immediately and intimately connected, the penal injury to the soul manifested itself instantaneously in the flesh (13.13). "There appeared in their body a certain indecent novelty which made nakedness shameful," Augustine writes, "and made them self-conscious and embarrassed" (14.17; cf. 13.3, on Adam's experience of "rebellion and disobedience of desire in his body"; cf. Gen 3.7). This basic disjuncture of body and soul, enacted every time the human pair had sexual intercourse, echoed a further disjuncture with which every generation of the species would also be cursed: the soul, created by nature together with the flesh would be wrenched, unwilling, from the body at death. "Death drives the soul from the body against her will" (*City of God* 21.3). Death itself, a direct consequence of the Fall, is the ultimate manifestation of the will's broken power.

This reading of Genesis also provided Augustine with a way to theorize *how* Adam's sin was passed along from one generation to the next. Ancient medical science took conception as dependent on orgasm's "heating" the seed (both male and female) to produce the embryo. Augustine theologized this moment. Before the Fall, orgasm would have been volitional, and uncompromised by shame-producing pleasure. After the Fall, however, conception depended precisely on the radical enfeeblement of the rational mind's control over the body at the moment of orgasm. In this way, the infant, body and soul, comes into being as a *tradux peccati*, literally a "branch of sin." Christ, in contrast, was sinless both body and soul because he was born apart from normal human reproduction. His flesh he took from Mary, who conceived as a virgin; his soul came from the same source as Adam's—namely, God. Unlike other humans, then, Christ was free to love God and others with complete selflessness; he enjoyed a union of love and will unknown since Eden. Through his sinless incarnation, Christ revealed to humanity both how they should have been—but after the Fall could no longer be—and how, after, the resurrection, they would be: sinlessly and harmoniously united in flesh and spirit, body and soul.[21]

The sacrament of baptism (given even to infants) and the doctrine of the church (outside of which there is no salvation) affirmed Augustine's view of the transmission of original sin.

Reasoning backward from the universal necessity of salvation in Christ to the condemnation of all persons—even infants—unless baptism intervene, Augustine concluded that the reason for this condemnation could only have proceeded from Adam, the origin of the entire race and, thus, the font of original sin. Original sin, through the just judgment of God, causes each person to be born of the *massa perditionis*, literally, the "condemned lump"—a reference to Paul and to Romans 9.21–23, the *massa* of clay from which God the potter shapes humankind (*City of God* 21.12).

In light of this human material, is it any wonder that the social life of fallen humankind is so blighted by strife, injustice, incessant war? The citizens of the earthly city, the city of man, impacted in their own self-love, constantly war against the citizens of the heavenly city, those who love God, as they sojourn in time. It had ever been thus, since the founder of the earthly city, Cain, slew Abel, representative of the city of God (15.1). But the earthly city also wars incessantly within and against itself: "The human race, more than any other species, is at once social by nature and quarrelsome by perversion," (12.21; on power relations more generally, see 19.7–17). Lust for power (*libido dominandi*) characterizes all human societies, whether pagan or Christian, whether small or large. "What are kingdoms but large robber bands? What are robber bands but small kingdoms?" (4.4). Even the church itself, before the End, is a *corpus permixtum*, a society made up of a mixed population, containing both the reprobate and the good (18.49). Peace without war, society without power relations, can and will come only at history's end, when human nature, vitiated by the Fall, is itself healed and perfected in the final resurrection.

But who of the human family will be in this society of saints? What happens to those not elected to salvation? If all humanity is universally trapped in its condition of sin so that none can will effectively *not* to sin, if it is God alone who gives only to some sinners the grace to be able not to sin, then on what basis does God make his decision? And why, if he is all good and all powerful, did he permit things to happen as they did, condemning all humanity for Adam's transgression?

In the 390s, just preceding his writing of the *Confessions*, Augustine had considered these questions against the challenge of the Manichees. The Manichees had argued that the good god does *only* good. Anything bad—including sin—must accordingly proceed from another power opposed to and independent of God. (If this malicious power were not independent of God, God would be complicit in the operation of evil.) Lived experience attested to the cosmic conflict between two independent and opposed realms, Light and Darkness, Good and Evil. And the human being was a miniature instance of this intense battle. His moral failings reflected the strength of the forces of Darkness waging war within him—"the law of my members," as Paul had written, "at war with the law of my mind" (Rm 7.23–25). People sinned not because they wanted to, said the Manichees, but because they were forced to: they sinned because they were overcome by Sin.[22]

In arguing against the Manichees in defense of the will's freedom and of a god who was just as well as good, Augustine, like Origen before him, had had to consider Paul's statements in Romans 9. How could a just god first harden Pharaoh, then punish him? How could he fairly choose Jacob over Esau if neither had done anything whether good or bad because both were still in the womb? (Unlike Origen, Augustine invokes no precorporeal moral choice to explain the twins' separate fates; cf. p. 109.) How indeed can God justly hold sinners accountable, or justly reward those who do not sin, if both sides serve completely at his prerogative, the human pots to the divine potter?

It was within this context that Augustine first interpreted all humanity as *massa luti* or *massa perditionis* or *massa peccati*—a "lump of clay," a "lump of perdition," or a "lump of sin," referring to the clay from which God the potter shapes his pots in Romans 9.21. In framing this idea in his match against the Manichees, Augustine deployed the idea of free will as a queen gambit: after Adam, will was no longer free in a first-order way. Human will is free only to sin; but this is because of the soul's own misordered loves, not because of some overwhelming and evil external force (as the Manichees taught). After Adam, Augustine urged, all humanity is condemned; indeed, condemnation is all anyone deserves: "Sinful humanity must pay a debt of punishment to the supreme divine justice" (*To Simplicianus* 1.2,16). Thus God "hardens" Pharaoh by leaving Pharaoh in his sinful state. God does nothing to actively harm him, he simply does not help him (1.2,15–18). The same with Esau: God does no harm, he just does not help.

In light of humanity's universal sinfulness, indeed, the question becomes not, How is God just in condemning Esau? but, How is God just in redeeming Jacob? How, if both were equally "sinful," did God judge between them at all? Augustine's answer is, God only knows. Piety demands that the believer assert that God *must* have had good reason, but those reasons are known only to him: they are *occultissimi*, "most hidden." *Aequitate occultissima et ab humanis sensibus remotissima iudicat*: "He judges by a standard of justice most hidden and distant from human measure" (*To Simplicianus* 1.2,16). We can never know why God does what he does, why he saves one sinner rather than another. Do people have a hard time with God's inscrutability? "Who are you, O man, to answer back to God?" (1.2,18, quoting Paul in Rm 9.20).

In *City of God*, Augustine invokes this divine inscrutability to account for all of salvation history. Why did God allow the rebel angels to revolt? Why create humanity, if he foreknew that sin would be the result? Why proceed at all, if so much of his creation would be doomed to eternal punishment? "This was God's decision; a just decree, however inscrutable to us," counsels Augustine. "For Scripture says, 'All the Lord's ways are mercy and truth' (Ps 25.10). His grace cannot be unjust; nor can his justice be unkind" (*City of God* 12.28). We can neither see nor know *how* God is just; we can only affirm by faith that he is just. If out of pure mercy God chooses to save some from their justly deserved penalty of eternal damnation, then the only appropriate and pious response is to be grateful for his compassion.

But whom does God save from sin, whom does he relinquish to sin? Augustine answers,

> The whole of mankind is a *massa perditionis*, a condemned lump, for he who committed the first sin was punished, and along with him all the stock which had its roots in him. The result is that there is no escape for anyone from this justly deserved punishment, except by merciful and undeserved grace. Humanity is divided between those in whom the power of merciful grace is demonstrated, and those in whom is shown the might of just retribution. Neither of these could be displayed in respect of all mankind, for if all had remained condemned . . . then God's merciful grace would not have been seen . . . and if all had been transferred from darkness to light, then the truth of God's vengeance would not have been made evident. *Many more*

are condemned by vengeance than are released by mercy.
(21.12)

Thus Augustine dedicates the penultimate book of this long work, *City of God* 21, to an exploration of eternal condemnation. Both the wicked and the saved will be raised in their physical bodies at the end-time, he asserts. The question then becomes: Can a fleshly body endure pain that is eternal (21.3)? Can it burn forever, without being consumed (21.2)? Yes indeed, Augustine responds: since raised flesh will be constituted differently from the way flesh currently is, God will arrange hell so that "the worm will never die and the fire never go out." This will be achieved by "a miracle done by the omnipotent Creator" (21.9).

But are these punishments not temporary, endured as a process of purification? Maybe they are temporary for some people, Augustine concedes, but not for most (21.13). Perhaps, then, punishment will not last forever? "I am aware that I now have to engage in a debate . . . with those compassionate Christians who refuse to believe that the punishment of hell will be everlasting," he responds. "On this subject the most compassionate of all was Origen, who believed that the Devil himself and his angels will be rescued from their torments" (21.17). But this opinion is perverse, says Augustine: it contradicts the express words of God. Satan and his minions are irredeemable; and all humanity, certainly, will not be saved—not through the intercession of the saints (21.18), not through membership in the true church (21.20), not through the grace of the sacraments (21.25). Hell is hell. Its torments are its purpose. It lasts forever.

What then of those few, those happy few, whom God in his mysterious judgment elects to salvation? How does Augustine interpret their final redemption? As he moves on to this topic, the theme of the final book of *City of God*, Augustine evokes the old Jewish prophecies in Isaiah and in Daniel that speak of the establishment of God's kingdom, and of the renewed Jerusalem as the seat of the saints (22.2).

Centuries earlier Justin Martyr, reflecting on these and similar verses, had affirmed that the saints would be raised in their fleshly bodies, that they would gather in Jerusalem, and that they would reign there with Christ for a thousand years (*Trypho* 80–81; see pp. 89–90). Augustine, like Justin, is also committed to the idea of the resurrection of the flesh; and he, too, holds that the thousand-year reign of the saints occurs on earth. But Augustine's interpretation of these traditions differs sharply from that of Justin, and from the traditions of Christian (and especially of North African) millenarianism more generally. The kingdom is indeed linked to Christ's return in the body, he claims; but that event had already occurred centuries earlier, back in the first generation of the apostles, when the church— which is the body of Christ—arrived at Pentecost (20.6–9). The saints (especially through their bodily relics) reign with Christ, through the church, on earth, and they shall do so for 1000 years (20.9). But 1000 is a symbol, not a quantity: as 10 x 10 x 10, it represents wholeness or completion, it does not enumerate years (20.6). Thus the saints' reign will endure "for a thousand years," meaning until the times are fulfilled, whenever that might be (20.9). Only then, at this unknown and unknowable future date, will the final resurrection take place and the separation of the saved from the damned occur.

Can flesh be saved? Like Paul and like so many later ancient Christians of all persuasions, Augustine interpreted *flesh* as a shorthand term for sin: like *spirit*, *flesh* functioned very frequently as a moral category. Through the Fall, the human soul was made "fleshly," subject to sin; and ever since that point, humans have loved and lived *carnaliter* and *secundum carnem*, "according to the flesh," in the Pauline locution. But at the bodily resurrection, teaches Augustine, human flesh will be made "spiritual"—that is, utterly freed from sin, totally directed to and by spirit. In other words, Augustine can insist with Paul that the fleshly body will be raised spiritual (1 Cor 15.44), but "spiritual" for Augustine (unlike for Paul) refers only to the body's moral orientation, *not* to its substance: the raised body, for Augustine, will still be made of flesh (13.20; 22.21; 22.24). Christ's own resurrection in the flesh, he states, is the prototype of the believer's (18.46). The raised body will also be like Christ's in stature—that is, the person will be raised as he was in his prime (22.15). This raised body, further, will be physically perfect: people fat now will not be fat then, nor people thin now thin then (22.19). Amputees will have their limbs restored (22.20). The raised body will even be gendered: woman will rise as woman (22.17; there had obviously been some debate on this issue). And heaven holds no children: in the transformation of resurrection, even infants will be raised as mature adults (22.14).

Flesh, precisely because it so much serves as Augustine's premier synecdoche for sin, stands at the very center of his theology, focusing the fundamentals of Christian doctrine. Its maker was God himself, who had pronounced flesh "good" (the doctrine of creation); it was truly and fully assumed by God the Son (the doctrine of the incarnation); at the end of time, as foretold by Christ's own risen body, it will be redeemed (the doctrine of resurrection). Indeed, the central mystery and message of Christianity, Augustine insists, is the redemption of the flesh.

This conviction propelled several of Augustine's original and creative approaches to the Bible. His theology of time and language had already relativized the Bible's text. God's Word, once incarnate in the written word, represented scripture's fundamental translation from the timelessness of the divine realm (*Confessions* 11.7,9) into the historical contingencies—and maddening uncertainties—of human language (see p. 119). About the differences and even the discrepancies between the Bible's ancient Hebrew and the Septuagint's Greek, accordingly, Augustine shows remarkable sangfroid. He acknowledges these forthrightly, and even speaks of the Septuagint translators' mistakes (*City of God* 15.10). Sometimes, he holds, these mistakes or differences were prompted by the Holy Spirit, so that the Greek text might foretell a Christian truth where the Hebrew would not—a good reason not to correct the Greek text by looking at the Hebrew (18.43; Jerome, who made a new translation of the Old Testament from Hebrew into Latin, would not have appreciated the sentiment). The most important thing to remember when interpreting no matter which Biblical text, however, claimed Augustine, was to keep the books' historical witness in view: limitless spiritual interpretations notwithstanding, the Bible first of all offers "a faithful record of historical fact" (13.22; cf. 15.27, on allegorical and historical significance). And virtually reversing Origen's teaching, Augustine holds that while not every verse in the Bible has an allegorical meaning, every verse does have a historical meaning (17.4; cf. p. 111 in the present volume).

Augustine's commitment to scripture's historical witness led him to astounding novelty on the issue of Jewish blood sacrifices. The probity of these sacrifices had simply been assumed by most late Second Temple Jews, Jesus and Paul among them. To the degree that the eucharistic traditions go back to the historical Jesus, to that degree we can conjecture that he valued sacrifice so much that he used it as a prime analogy to his own work. And Paul had so esteemed the temple cult that he presented Christ himself both as a temple sacrifice and as a temple priest (see p. 36), and he used temple protocols to provide a guiding metaphor for understanding how God was integrating baptized pagans into Israel's impending redemption (see p. 38). The gospel writers themselves, in the generation or so following Jesus and Paul, also presented Jesus as a type of sacrifice for sin (see p. 22). The temple in Jerusalem, the biblical legislation on purification and offerings, the cultural presumptions about the way that sacrifices work to effect atonement: these are the *fundamenta* of the earliest traditions' presentation of Jesus and of his mission.[23]

Second-century gentile Christians, on the other hand, decades after the Roman destruction of Jerusalem, rebuked Jews for having ever indulged in anything so blatantly "pagan" as blood sacrifices. God had instituted his own sacrificial protocols in the wake of the incident with the Golden Calf, taught Justin Martyr, only as "an accommodation, . . . so that you would not serve idols" (*Trypho* 19). The matrix of the blood sacrifice was pagan worship, pagan culture, said these theologians; it had never been appropriate to the worship of the true god. And the Jews, interpreting the laws of sacrifice in a fleshly way (that is, by actually offering animals) rather than spiritually, as allegories of Christ, enacted their own religious wrongheadedness, indicting themselves as a sinful, carnal people (*Trypho* 13, 15–16, 27, and frequently; see pp. 88 and 97 infra.).

By reading the Bible *ad litteram,* "historically," Augustine turned this anti-Jewish trope on its head. The Bible did not dissemble, he insisted. If it portrayed God as commanding these offerings, then these offerings are what God had wanted, and they had been appropriate and good. But why? Since God obviously has no need of sacrifices, says Augustine, their purpose must have been pedagogical. God had wanted "to teach us something that would be good for us to know, which was suitably symbolized by these offerings" (*Against Faustus* 6.5). And what was this lesson? That his Son would come in the flesh, and purify humankind through his own blood (18.6; 22.21). Jewish blood sacrifices, understood historically, prefigured substantially the incarnate Christ's sacrifice of himself.

Justin had said much the same, but he had drawn the further lesson that Christ *alone* was the true sacrifice; Jewish sacrifices, he therefore concluded, were wrong (see p. 97). If Justin's was an either/or approach, Augustine's was both/and. Jesus was the true blood sacrifice prefigured by the Jewish ones, and the Jews had been *right* to interpret the laws of sacrifice *secundum carnem*. In this way the Jews not only preserved God's prophetic word in his book; they also *enacted* the prophecy *historically*, pronouncing the truth of the Incarnation *ad litteram*, through their actions (*Against Faustus* 12.9, 14.6, and frequently). But then what of the undeniable resemblance of Jewish blood sacrifices to pagan ones? They looked similar, argued Augustine, not because Jews had imitated pagan rituals, but because malicious demons, demanding worship from pagans, misled them by sacrilegiously imitating the divinely established Jewish rites (20.18). Besides, the Bible had already shown historically through the example of Abel that blood sacrifice had been pleasing to God since humanity's very beginnings (22.17; Gen 4.4). Blood, Augustine taught, whether that of the temple cult or that specifically and finally of the incarnate Christ, really does achieve atonement for sin.[24]

But Christ had done more than come in the flesh, and die in the flesh: to redeem the flesh, he had also been raised in the flesh and—more astonishingly still—he had ascended into heaven with his flesh (*City of God* 18.46). Heaven, too, is the goal of the resurrected Christian. In defiance both of traditions of Christian millenarianism (which had expected a terrestrial redemption) and of the scientific thinking of his day (the weight of the elements, 13.18; the organization of the cosmos, 22.4; 22.11), Augustine insists that final redemption will *not* come on earth. It will be in heaven, to which will ascend the saints in their restored and perfected bodies—"possessing the substance of the flesh, but untainted by any carnal corruption." There they will experience the greatest possible joy: the unmediated knowledge of God. No more words. No more books. No more interpretation. In eternity, no more time: "Knowledge without error, entailing no toil! For we shall drink of God's Wisdom [Christ] at its very source, with supreme felicity, without any difficulty" (22.24).

In heaven, flesh without sin. Humanity will have moved from Adam's first state, being equally able to sin (*posse peccare*) and not to sin (*posse non peccare*), through Adam's fallen state, not being able not to sin (*non posse non peccare*), to possessing a greater degree of freedom than Adam ever did, not being able to sin (*non posse peccare*)—not because the will is not free, Augustine insists, but because the will "will be the freer in that it is freed from a delight in sin and immovably fixed in a delight of not sinning" (22.30). As for Origen, then, and as for the traditions of Greek moral philosophy that both draw on, so also for Augustine: the truly free will chooses only the good.

Much still distinguishes their respective views of eternal redemption. For Origen, redeemed rational beings form a radically egalitarian "society," since the scrupulously fair God had made all souls in the atemporal beginning "out of one lump," with the selfsame ability to freely choose (see p. 108). Augustine's heavenly society has gender, ranks, and status. People who were virgins, or who were martyrs, will have a higher "grade of honor" than those who were not. The eschatological miracle will be that no one feels envy of the higher-ups: unlike in the old earthly city, "organization will be harmonious" (22.30). The scope of redemption is much wider for Origen, who reckons the whole embodied higher cosmos, not only humanity, as the object of Christ's saving mission; for Augustine, the sole focus of Christ's mission was humanity alone.

Perhaps the greatest difference between Origen and Augustine is the temperament of their respective gods. Origen's god loves his entire creation, and acts to save every individual being. Augustine's god, justly angry at sin, redeems only a small number of people, just enough to display his mercy (21.12). But as with Origen, so also Augustine: the return of the soul to the One—the great destiny of the wise soul in late Platonism—is refracted through Paul's eschatological vision in 1 Corinthians 15.28. In the End, "God will be all things to everyone" (*City of God* 22.30).

EPILOGUE

Ancient ideas about sin provide a point of orientation from which
we can move out to examine other concept clusters that defined
early forms of Christianity. Who is saved from sin, and how?
What texts and concepts define both what sin is and how to deal
with it? How does sin define redemption? And what, finally, do
ideas of sin tell us about corresponding ideas of humanity, and
of God?

The seven figures we have examined both converge and
diverge in their answers to these questions. The two earliest,
Jesus and Paul, spoke to different audiences. Jesus focused on
fellow Jews for his mission, Paul focused on pagans. Accordingly, each dealt with different ideas of sin. For Jesus as for his
hearers, sin is "Jewish" sin, primarily, breaking the (ten) commandments. Jesus teaches ways to avoid doing that, especially
in Matthew's Sermon on the Mount (see p. 16); and he also
teaches that repentance restores the Jew to good relations with
his fellows, and with God. The specific spur to this message—
itself cohering with Jesus' native religious tradition—was his
conviction that the god of Israel was about to establish his king-

Figure 5. Christus Militans. This beautiful beardless young man, dressed as a Roman soldier (perhaps as an emperor) is a sixth-century representation of the Christ of imperial Christianity. The mosaic visually proclaims theological points of principle. The figure treads on a lion and a snake, recalling a line from Psalm 91.3, while the script proclaims its identity as the Johannine Christ: "I am the way, the truth, and the life" (John 14.6). In this way, the image binds together the Old Testament and the New around the figure of Jesus, whose military garb in turn proclaims the relation of church and empire. (Note how delicately the mosaic refers to Jesus' crucifixion!) This late Roman political symbiosis of religious authority and imperial power combined to disallow contemporary religious diversity; to disenfranchise pagans, Jews, and Christian minorities; and to "rewrite" the history of Christian origins. Photo courtesy Erich Lessing/Art Resource, New York. Museo Arcivescovile, Ravenna, Italy.

dom. Who would enter? Those Jews who harkened to Jesus' teachings and who accepted his authority to announce the kingdom's advent would enter before those Jews who rejected them. When would the kingdom come? Very soon. Where would it come? If we can extrapolate from Jesus' sayings about drinking wine in the kingdom, and from the postresurrection activity of his disciples, the kingdom would come on earth, in Jerusalem. The god of Israel receives repentant sinners, Jesus taught; and in that gracious forgiveness, God gave an example of how Jesus' followers should treat each other.[1]

The mission's segue to pagans came only after Jesus' lifetime. As we saw when looking at Paul, "gentile" sin—also defined by appeal to Jewish scripture—is imagined differently from "Jewish" sin. Gentiles worship gods other than Israel's god, and they do so by recourse to idols. The traditional Jewish rhetoric against such worship that Paul mobilizes deals at lavish length with the sins attendant on idol worship: theft, adultery, murder, and (especially) fornication (see p. 25f.). Gentiles who want a place in God's coming kingdom—now linked for Paul as for other early apostles with the second coming of Christ—enter through baptism into Christ; thereby infused with *pneuma*, divine spirit, they renounce their idols, withhold cult to false gods, and live according to idealized Jewish ethics (see p. 46).

Who populates the kingdom once it comes? Again, Jesus seems to have spoken primarily to and about Israel; but the mission that formed around his message and memory so readily accommodated itself to a gentile mission that we are justified in assuming that Jesus placed himself within the broader, more universalist streams of Jewish apocalyptic hope. The kingdom's demography would reflect that of the preredeemed world: it would contain both gentiles and Jews. To this same question

Paul gives a two-stage answer: first, now, in the proleptic kingdom represented by the *ekklēsia*, those pagans who listen to Paul, and those Jews who agree with Paul ("a remnant chosen by grace"); but, ultimately, all Israel and the full number of gentiles. In the End, God, the just and merciful sovereign of human history, will make good both on his promises to Israel ("for the gifts and the calling of God are irrevocable"), and on his promise to Abraham concerning the gentiles (who, as Abraham was, are "made righteous through faith.")

Human redemption from sin, in short, is imagined and presented on a much bigger scale in Paul's letters than in the synoptic gospels, whose Jesus stays focused primarily if not exclusively on the redemption of Israel. But Pauline redemption is on a much bigger scale in any case: Paul expects celestial powers, the lower cosmic gods of pagan pantheons, to cease their rebellion against the god of Israel and also, finally, to kneel to their conqueror, his Son; and Sin itself, as a cosmic force, will be utterly vanquished along with Flesh and Death (1 Cor 15.26; Romans 8, passim). Christ the triumphant cosmic warrior will establish his Father's kingdom, but for Paul, unlike for Jesus, that kingdom seems located not on earth, but "in the air" (1 Thes 4.17), to which will ascend the spiritual bodies of redeemed humanity. When will these things happen? Soon, Paul believes; very very soon.

Though many ancient Christians continued to hold a vivid belief in the imminent End throughout the four centuries that we review (indeed, many modern Christians hold it still), the later gentile theologians whose work we have studied did not. Instead, they transposed redemption into a different key, whether emphasizing the individual spiritual ascent of the saved believer after death (Valentinus, Marcion, Origen), or holding to an eschatological end-time that was in principle unknowably distant (Justin, Origen again, Augustine). And, with the conspicuous exception of Origen, none kept Paul's vision of universal redemption, whether human or cosmic. All sketched their idea of sin from the biblical template—or, in Marcion's case, from that biblical template as mediated particularly by Pauline tradition—but their assessment of sin's root causes differed, as did their ideas of who were redeemed, and how.[2]

Both Valentinus and, with a difference, Justin construed sin as a function of ignorance: the sinner sinned because he did not know God's will, both a cause and an effect of which was not reading the Septuagint with "spiritual" insight (meaning, with the correct allegorical or mystical interpretation). Adapting Paul's terminology, Valentinus restricted redemption, thus correct reading, to those with the ability to receive revelation, the "spirituals" (*pneumatikoi*) and the "soulish" (*psuchikoi*). Does one achieve such ability through effort—in other words, does free will come into play?—or is such ability innate? Valentinus' Christian opponents criticized him for leaving no scope for free will. The accusation implied that Valentinus had no concept of virtue; it was a short step from there to accusing Valentinians of having no morals. Such polemic tells us nothing about actual Valentinians; and we do know from Ptolemy's letter to Flora that the Ten Commandments figured in their spirituality and ethics (see p. 68). The whole visible, material cosmos, further, as well as those people who could not or did not receive saving knowledge (*hulikoi*, "material people"), stood outside the scope of spiritual redemption. We may conjecture that this human population included pagans and Jews as well as unknowing Christians.

Justin similarly emphasized the importance of (correct) knowledge. People invariably behave badly, and thus sin, if they have an incorrect notion of God; conversely, the correct notion of God (that is, Justin's notion) leads to virtuous behavior. Pagans as well as Christian competitors fall into the category "sinners." So, emphatically, do most Jews, who have obdurately misread their own scriptures and failed to realize that the active deity portrayed there is Justin's savior, the preincarnate Son. At work in these lost populations Justin sees demonic agency, and he warns that the demons, who as rational beings also have free will, will be judged no less harshly than will these human sinners.

Flesh codes for sin, functioning for Justin as for Paul (and for all of these later Christian writers) as an ethical antipode of *spirit*. But *flesh* for Justin particularly codes in negative ways for *Jewish*. Justin accordingly claims the Jewish scriptures for his gentile church by de-ethnicizing them, divorcing them through allegorical interpretation from traditionally Jewish understandings. Through their ancestral practices—circumcision and blood sacrifices, most of all—the Jews, Justin insists, have literally enacted their misreading of the texts in their characteristic "fleshly" way. As did the prophets before him and the apostles and Justin's church after him, Jesus himself preached against the fleshly Jewish understanding of Jewish law. Understood spiritually—the way it was intended to be understood—the Septuagint is the witness to and charter for Justin's gentile church. Redeemed flesh, however, made immortal (thus free of sin) by Christ and conferred on the saved at the resurrection of the saints, will inherit the adorned eschatological Jerusalem "as Ezekiel, Isaiah, and others declare" (*Trypho* 80)—a "fleshly" vision that would surely strike Valentinus and Marcion as very "Jewish"!

For Justin the philosopher, then, sin's root reason is intellectual: it results from a misapprehension of the divine. Christ the Logos guides the virtuous (including even those pagan philosophers, like Socrates, who managed, mutatis mutandis, to conceptualize divinity appropriately). Christ the *heteros theos*, the "other god," speaks through the Septuagint to those who interpret the text correctly. Christ the incarnate Son fulfills the prophecies of the scriptures, thereby demonstrating the truth of Justin's reading; at his second coming, he will vindicate this reading by fulfilling those prophecies outstanding. Far above the fray, meanwhile, "the nameless god" (1 *Apology* 53), God the Father, the nonethnic, radically transcendent high god of philosophical paideia, presides over all.

Finally, our two premier biblical theologians, Origen and Augustine, understand sin both universally and individually. Sin on the one hand represents a universal condition or situation that one is born into: the structure of the material cosmos or the universal limitations imposed by human nature testify to the global effects of an ancient, prehistoric fall. On the other hand, both men understand sin as an episode in the life of an individual primarily in terms drawn from late Platonism. This sin, individual sin, is a turning away from God; its occasion is the freedom of the will. Sin begins not with ignorance but with choice. But why does the will make bad choices?

Origen, as we have seen, imagines sin's origins in the variable responses of contingent but eternal spiritual beings who turned away "from" God (metaphorically understood: in the immaterial cosmos, there was no extension or direction). This turning away or lapse in itself was not culpable. But, claims Origen, these rational beings' letting themselves (continue to) slip from God was "irrational," a "failure to adhere to the ends and ordinances laid down by reason." It is this "departure from what is just and right" that is sin (*On First Principles* I. v, 2). In other words, these creatures' sin was not the Fall itself: since they are contingent beings, dependent upon God for their own existence, they could not help but waver. It was their allowing themselves to fall some "distance" before *choosing* to stop that was their sin. Such behavior—knowingly lapsing from God—is unreasonable. The will makes bad choices when it acts against reason; unreason leads to sin.

Augustine, reading Genesis *ad litteram*, seems at first blush to derive his idea of sin more immediately from the biblical story itself. He imagines original sin as a discrete moment, the act of Adam who, as a single, historical, embodied human being, freely decided to disobey the divine command. Augustine parses this moment of decision minutely in book 14 of *City of God*. Before that moment, Adam and Eve had enjoyed "a serene avoidance of sin" (14.10). And the command, once given, was easily kept, since "it was given at a time when desire was not yet in opposition to the will" (14.12). But after Eve was beguiled by the serpent, Adam chose to join with her, perhaps convinced that the transgression was really venial (14.13). His "evil will"— a type of pride, putting his own desires above God's—preceded his evil act.

But *why* was Adam's will so susceptible to fault? Augustine the Neoplatonist answers, "Only a nature created out of nothing could have been distorted by a fault. Consequently, though the will derives its existence as a nature from its creation by God, *its falling away from its true being is due to its creation out of nothing*" (14.13). Created nature, in other words, is intrinsically unstable. We are back in Origen's universe, where contingency opens the pathway to sin.

If sin, for both theologians, is the departure from God and the good, the mind's kinship with God, through the free exercise of the will, provides the royal road back. No contemporary pagan philosopher of Platonic bent would disagree with this idea: Plotinus, indeed, was its source for Augustine. Origen fills out this idea of sin and redemption, fall and return, with explicitly Christian teachings. The way back to God, he says, is aided by (secondary) creation, the material cosmos providentially arranged by the Father through the Son; by the scriptures, especially when interpreted with spiritual understanding; and by the teachings of the true (that is, Origen's) church (*On First Principles* I, passim). Augustine, by contrast, alters this idea significantly through his understanding of original sin, the consequence of Adam's fall, "the . . . inheritance of sin and death conveyed to us by birth" (*City of God* 13.23). Original sin mitigates the will's freedom for the primal parents, and for every generation thereafter. Who, then, is saved from sin and death? Only those few whose will God's grace has "healed." Being a member of the true (that is, Augustine's) church is a necessary precondition to receiving such healing, but not a sufficient one. Salvation—the turn from sin and return to God—depends upon the inscrutable decision *of* God.

It is in their respective ideas about God that Origen and Augustine finally differ so much, and so characteristically, from each other. The high god of each represents a genuine and intimate fusion of biblical and philosophical ideas. But where they hold their philosophical ideas in common—the deity's radical transcendence, his changeless perfection and goodness, his timelessness, his utter incorporeality—they each draw on different features of their common biblical heritage. This is nowhere more evident than in their reading of Paul's letter to the Romans, particularly chapters 9–11, where Paul celebrates God's sovereignty in history and reveals the *musterion* of coming universal redemption.

Origen kept much of Paul's emotional tone and happy conviction, filling in the details with his own commitments to God's ethical transparency. As he works through the biblical episodes reviewed in this swatch of Romans in book III of *On First Principles*, Origen exegetically shifts the decisive agency from God to humankind. Thus, God chose Jacob over Esau before either was born because the twins' respective souls had made different moral choices before they had life in the body. God's "hardening" Pharaoh's heart actually meant that Pharaoh had hardened his own heart. Human "pots" make themselves into vessels of honor or dishonor by their own unimpeded moral choices (see p. 107f.). This switch of agency preserved the soul's free will, and therefore the justice of God. Election in the historical sphere as recounted in scripture, insisted Origen, spoke to God's morally coherent recognition of individual merit.

Behind Origen's interpretation, and supporting it, lay two prime a priori convictions. The first—that rational beings make moral choices before they live in the fleshly body—preserved the justice of divine judgment, a core defining feature of the biblical god (*On First Principles* II. v, 1). For the opposite of justice is not mercy; the opposite of justice is arbitrariness. God's judgments, claimed Origen, gesturing toward eternity, were not arbitrary; they can only seem so when one forgets that life in the material body is but one small episode in the infinitely long life of the soul. This conviction, further, also squared the circle bequeathed to all Christian theologians by their double inheritance of biblical narrative and philosophical paideia: how does a timeless, unchanging deity "create"? Origen's eternally generated spiritual creation addressed this problem, protecting the biblical god's philosophical credentials: God "creates" without effort, eternally, before the existence of matter and time; lower, material creation is the work of his Logos. And given that this foregoing spiritual universe was the essential arena of the souls' moral choices, it also protected the philosophical god's biblical credentials: God is *both* merciful *and* just.

This last claim about God's justice and mercy was further supported by Origen's second a priori conviction: God loves his whole creation equally, from the rational soul of Jesus to the rational soul of Satan, and everyone else's in between. (Nothing less would be fair, thus just.) This means that God wants his whole creation to be happy. And since happiness lies solely in loving God (itself another principle in which the Bible and late Platonism converge), this in turn means that Origen's god actively wants to redeem his whole creation, returning it to himself: his justice and mercy attest to his *goodness*. Since he is God, he will get his way. Origen's lengthy peregrination through Greek moral philosophy and metaphysical cosmology, in short, lands him back at Paul's happy ending: God will save everyone—stars, planets, demons, humans, the entire ensouled fellowship of the universe. Anything less would not only be unjust; it would not cohere with God's essential goodness.

What of Augustine's god? Whom does he save, and why? The theater of salvation is much more narrowly restricted for Augustine, in two senses: first, humanity alone is the focus of redemption and, second, only some small portion of humanity at that. How is this portion chosen? Augustine, like Origen, worries about God's seeming arbitrary: divine choice *must* be morally coherent, made for a good reason. And so it is, he insists. But no one can know how: divine choice *in principle* is not morally transparent. What to the historical Paul, in Romans 9–11, is the unexpected and surprising way that God is about to redeem Jew and gentile both, for Augustine is the hidden mystery of the way that God chooses between one sinner and the other, saving one but not the other. And the hardening of Israel that Paul in Romans 11.25 claims is temporary and providential Augustine interprets as penal and permanent. And somehow, in some unknowable way, just.

Hence Augustine's mobilization of the word *occulta*, "hidden," or, more frequently, *occultissima*, "most hidden." The reasons for God's choice of Jacob over Esau are *occultissimi*. So are God's reasons for hardening Israel. In fact, all of God's reasons for making any of his judgments are *occultissimi*. All peoples—pagans, Jews, heretics, everyone—are part of the *massa damnata*, justly condemned because of Adam's sin. If God chooses to redeem some and condemn others, his reasons for doing so are inscrutable. Because he is God, those reasons must be just. Their justice, however, is most hidden. Why should God be concerned about his moral transparency to his own creatures? asked Augustine, with a nod to Romans 9.20 ("Who are you, O man, to answer back to God?"). Let humankind affirm God's justice by faith.[3]

～～～

Jesus of Nazareth, back in the early first century, had linked his call to repent from sin to his announcement of God's coming kingdom, thus history's eschatological finale. That clarion of the kingdom remained in Christian texts, appealed to by later believers who framed their own times with this message, and this message with their times. Four centuries after Jesus, rocked by the sack of Rome in 410, riven by long traditions of Christian millenarian calculations that named the period between the fifth and sixth centuries as the expected date for Christ's return, the Western world very nearly did "end" on time. In 430, Vandal invaders battered Augustine's Africa. Augustine himself, struck by fever, lay on his death bed—alone, reading penitential psalms, weeping for his sins, going to the inscrutable and angry god that he had created. Through the eyes of his first biographer, this is our last glimpse of him.[4]

Our aerial survey of the idea of sin in the first four Christian centuries ends here. We have seen its mutagenic, vibrant vitality. Our thinkers invoked sin to account for an astonishing range of things, from the physical structure of the universe to the grammatical structure of a sentence; from the death of God's son to the power politics of the empire that eventually worshiped him.

Have these ancient arguments, or their effects, lingered into our own period? The extreme variety of contemporary Christianity—even the extreme varieties within ostensibly one community, such as the Roman Catholic church—should instill a certain caution in trying to answer such a question. As a historian of antiquity, I speak with no academic authority about our own period. But since I look at our period through the intellectual prism of my historical knowledge, I can offer several observations—not about contemporary theology as such, but about contemporary, specifically American culture.

The discourse of modern wrongdoing, and of modern wrongdoers; current criminal law (influenced, as ever, by the identity and social status of the criminal); penitents publicly confessing their wicked, wicked ways, whether in the pages of *People* or on television's airwaves: I am struck by the ways that ostensible acknowledgments of culpability minimize or even efface personal agency, thus responsibility. Sometimes these "acknowledgments" invoke a trope once sounded by Platonism, wherein "sin" (or its secular manifestation, "crime") is really "error." People do not commit crimes (much less "sin"!); they blunder. "Mistakes were made," says a president, using the bureaucratic passive voice (thereby nicely obscuring agency, too: the sentence does not continue, "by me"). But even in active-voice confessions, the language of "mistakes" attenuates the agent's connection to his own action. "I made a mistake" has a quite different quality from "I did something wrong." Plus, how can anyone punish anyone for making a mistake? *Everyone* makes mistakes.[5]

"Sin" and its various historical entailments—guilt, remorse, judgment, punishment, penance, atonement—seem to sit athwart contemporary sensibilities. This perhaps explains why many modern readers, both professional scholars and college undergraduates, have reformatted two of our ancient figures, Jesus and Augustine, to better fit our culture's comfort zone. In some recent retellings, for example, the historical Jesus battles not ancient demons but modern ones: sexism, classism, elitism, even nationalism. The illnesses he combats are psychological, not physical. Sin? Jesus' god is a loving god, understanding, patient, forgiving. The call to repentance (repent of *what?*) recedes into the deep background as Jesus shrinks from being an apocalyptic prophet, an exorcist and healer and worker of mighty *paradoxa*, to being a premier culture critic and self-help guru.[6]

Augustine is another favored site for this sort anachronistic makeover. He himself is partly accountable, of course, having inadvertently facilitated modern misreadings by the way that he shaped his *Confessions*. His mother Monica, for example, looms large in the first nine books of his narrative. Given modernity's ubiquitous watered-down Freudianism, she can seem to flip an oedipal Augustine right onto the couch. Much of his anguish, accordingly, registers as sexual conflict, not helped by his constant recourse to a rich vocabulary of specifically sexual transgression. (*Caveat lector:* Augustine also describes his theft of pears when he was twelve years old as an act of *fornicatio*; *Confessions* 2.6,14. Clearly, he works here with ideas other than illicit sexual congress.) The intellectually tougher final 40 percent of the *Confessions*—the brilliant philosophical investigations into time and consciousness, epistemology, scriptural exegesis—usually go unread. Seduced by Augustine's narrative presentation into reading "psychologically" in the modern sense; assuming, from his title and from his obvious topic (sex!), that the book represents his "true confessions," many modern readers are relieved to find, in this fourth-century saint, some familiar version of a person they might see on *Oprah*: a "sex addict," not a sinner. He's too hard on himself. He should love himself more. He needs therapy, not repentance.

Comprendre tout, c'est pardonner tout: To understand everything is to excuse everything. And empathy, surely, is a virtue. But is it a virtue to so diminish individual agency, and thus the responsibility of the agent? Absent individual responsibility, it seems impossible to have a clear idea of crime, much less of sin.

Individual responsibility speaks to the human component of our classical three-way configuration of factors for conceiving an idea of sin: humanity, revealed knowledge, divinity. Acknowledged guidelines (for many of our thinkers, as we have seen, the role filled by revelation, often served by the Ten Commandments), speak to the component of revealed knowledge. But what about the third factor, divinity? Absent God—the notional condition of modern Western culture since Friedrich Nietzsche—is it possible for the idea of sin to have any traction at all? In theory, probably not. *But.* But we all live within the web of culture. And the biblical god (his many different denominational variations notwithstanding) seems to have taken up permanent residence in Western imagination, as one of his biographers has noted: even nonbelievers seem to know exactly who or what it is that they do not believe in. Perhaps sin fares likewise: People may not "believe" in sin, and they may be convinced that while they themselves might "make mistakes" they do not "really" sin; but they somehow seem to know sin when they see it in the behavior of others. Or perhaps what's really been lost, absent God, is not a coherent idea of sin so much as a coherent idea of redemption.[7]

The main point of the present volume is not to argue that the idea of "sin" requires an idea of "God." My main point is that ancient ideas of sin—as modern ideas of sin—are, like all human products, culturally constructed. Heavenly revelations may stand as their source; but since these revelations were either mediated by incarnate, temporally bounded individuals or were preserved and presented in texts—in Genesis and in Exodus, in the gospels, in Paul's letters—they are also read or heard, thus understood, by historically embedded human interpreters. "God," "the Bible," "the moral agent," as we have seen throughout the course of our study, have been imagined variously in Western definitions of sin, though these elements themselves have figured constantly. But, as we have also seen, time itself makes these constants *in*constant: historical context arbitrates meaning. At the end of the day, howsoever defined, "sin" suits its times.

Timeline

330s BCE	Conquests of Alexander the Great; Greek culture exported on large scale ("Hellenism")
200	Jewish scriptures translated into Greek (Septuagint, or LXX)
6	Birth of Jesus (Gospel of Matthew)
37–34	Reign of Herod the Great, King of the Jews

---

6 CE	Judea becomes Roman province
	Birth of Jesus (Gospel of Luke)
c. 28 (?)	execution of John the Baptist; beginning of Jesus' mission
c. 30 (?)	execution of Jesus of Nazareth in Jerusalem
c. 34 (?)	Jesus movement reaches Damascus; Paul persecutes, then joins the movement; mission to pagans
c. 50	Paul writes letters extant in New Testament collection (1 Thessalonians, Philemon, 1 and 2 Corinthians, Philippians, Galatians, Romans)
66	Outbreak of Jewish revolt against Rome

70	Roman destruction of Jerusalem, Temple of Jerusalem
c. 75–100	Gospels of Mark, Matthew, Luke, and John composed; Acts of the Apostles in late first/early second century; Josephus writes *Jewish War* and *Antiquities of the Jews*
130	fl. Valentinus (Alexandria, then Rome)
132–135	Bar Kokhba revolt in Judea; Rome changes name of province to "Palestine"
140	fl. Marcion (Pontus, then Rome)
150	fl. Justin Martyr (Palestine, then Rome)
190	fl. Tertullian (Carthage)
200	fl. Irenaeus (Lyons)
220–250	fl. Origen (Alexandria, then Caesarea in Palestine); dies in 254
280s	Mani spreads new Christian revelation (Persia, then throughout Near East and Mediterranean; along Silk Road into China)
312	Constantine becomes imperial patron of one sect of Christian church; secures power in Western Roman Empire
354	Augustine born in North Africa; converts to Manichaeism c. 373 in Carthage; converts to catholic Christianity 386–87 in Milan; becomes bishop of Hippo in 396
c. 400	Outbreak of empirewide controversy over Origen's theology
410	"Fall" of Rome to Visigoths
411–428	Augustine writes *City of God*
430	Vandals besiege Hippo; death of Augustine

Acknowledgments

My sincere thanks go, first of all, to the members of Princeton University's Committee on Public Lectures for their invitation to me to give the Spencer Trask Lectures in the fall of 2007. I also thank Peter Brown, John Gager, and Annemarie Luijendijk for their kind introductory remarks on that occasion; my intrepid listeners, who braved New Jersey's autumn rains to come to hear me; and my dear friend Sari Miller, who made a special effort to attend. Finally, I thank my husband Fred Tauber for listening so patiently while I fretted my way through this material, and for graciously making dinner so many more times than he should have had to.

Fred Appel, my editor at Princeton University Press, helped me to conceive the themes and to develop the ideas that went into those lectures and, thus, into this book. His enthusiasm, great intellectual clarity, and constant encouragement both buoyed me up and enabled me to bring the project to port. Thank you, Fred, for making *Sin* so much fun.

Two anonymous readers for the Press gave my penultimate draft much careful criticism, which enabled me to clarify both what I wanted to say and what I did not. I thank them warmly for their generous collegiality.

As I was completing this book in the summer of 2010, my beautiful, hilarious kid sister Lisa went to sleep one night and the next morning never woke up. Time tames the pain, but can never heal the loss. I miss her every day. In peace her sleep, and may her memory be for a blessing.

Notes

Author Note: Throughout this book I frequently use italics to emphasize certain words or passages in the texts quoted; all such emphases are my own.

Prologue

1. For a recent though very different treatment, spanning the Jewish scriptures in Hebrew to a classic of medieval Christian theology, Anselm's *Cur Deus Homo*, see Gary A. Anderson, *Sin: A History*. In that study, Anderson traces the shift in the Old Testament's metaphors for sin from "burden" to "debt," and then follows developments around that particular concept in the New Testament through to later rabbinic and Christian thought.

Chapter 1. God, Blood, and the Temple: Jesus and Paul on Sin

1. On John's role as Jesus' mentor, the most recent full study is John P. Meier, *A Marginal Jew*, 2.19–233; see, in short, Paula Fredriksen, *Jesus of Nazareth, King of the Jews*, 184–97. Dale C. Allison Jr., *Constructing Jesus*, 204–20, reviews *à la loupe* the similarities and differences between the two prophetic figures.

2. Meier, *A Marginal Jew*, argues that John's immersions were a one-time event (2:56), and that they "implicitly" challenged the traditional cultic means

of atonement and sacrifice at the temple (2:75, n.52). I question both of these conclusions. First, nothing in the gospel material—or in Josephus' report about John's activities (*Antiquities* 18.116–19)—indicates how many times a person could immerse, and common practice at the time was multiple immersions. (Even in the much later Christian context, when single immersions were desirable in principle, people might receive baptism a number of times: when moving between different Christian sects, for example; or if the authority and bona fides of the person administering the immersion were in question, as occurred during the fourth-century Donatist controversy.) Second, immersion was never a substitute for sacrifice; on this point, see Joan Taylor, *The Immerser*, 31, 95, 111.

On apocalyptic Jewish traditions about the Kingdom of God, and how these figure in traditions from and about John and Jesus, see E. P. Sanders, *Jesus and Judaism*, 77–119, 222–41. On purity, sacrifice, and atonement, see n. 11 below.

3. The gospels are composite documents, the final products of creative traditions (both oral and written) in which old material was reworked and new material added. Both Matthew and Luke, for example, independently rewrite Mark, while (again independently of each other) blending in material from other sources: the Greek version of the Jewish Bible, that is, the Septuagint; "Q," another Greek source—whether written or oral is hard to say—that conveys traditions about the Baptizer and about Jesus (mostly sayings; some stories); and finally other material, its origins now lost to us, that stems from their own individual communities. Different gospels and different sources have their own characteristic emphases. Much of the "Q" material, for example, dwells on apocalyptic judgment; Matthew, on Jesus' loyalty to the Law; Luke, on love and forgiveness. And the Gospel of John, like its own main character, is a type of mysterious stranger: lacking the kind of comparative grid for the Fourth Gospel that the synoptics' literary interrelations allows us to generate for them, its sources are much more obscure. Reconstructing Jesus from these later portraits requires patience and critical reading, and absolute certainty is simply not possible. For two introductory statements on the sources and the nature of this enterprise, see Paula Fredriksen, *From Jesus to Christ*, 3–8; and Fredriksen, *Jesus of Nazareth*, 18–34. On the ways that the temple's destruction affects—and should not affect—historical analyses of the New Testament materials, see Fredriksen, *Jesus of Nazareth*, 34–41.

4. The synoptic tradition presents Jesus' action in the temple toward the end of their gospels, since it serves as the trip-switch to the Passion. John uses the story very early on (Jn 2.13–22), where it obviously serves a different function. The historical authenticity of Jesus' temple gesture is current ortho-

doxy in New Testament studies; the gesture itself, however, is interpreted very variously. For a critique of the consensus, see Paula Fredriksen, "Markan Chronology, the Scene at the Temple, and the Death of Jesus"; on Mark's intertwining the themes of Jesus' death and the "death" of the temple, see Fredriksen, *From Jesus to Christ*, 44–52, 177–87.

5. All the recipients of Paul's letters seem to have been former pagans: "You turned to God from idols" (1 Thes 1.9; cf. 1 Cor 6.9); "therefore shun the worship of idols" (1 Cor 10.14); "When you did not know God, you were in bondage to beings who by nature are not gods" (Gal 4.8); "Look out for those who mutilate the flesh" (an intemperate reference to rival Christian missionaries, but the point is that only a male gentile could be a candidate for adult circumcision; Phil 3.2); "to bring about the obedience of faith for the sake of his name among all the gentiles, including you" (Rm 1.5–6). Romans also speaks of relations between Jews and gentiles, and for that reason some scholars have inferred that Paul's recipients there, too, are mixed; but I think not. (Caroline Johnson Hodge, *If Sons, then Heirs*, 9–11, gives a brisk review of the interpretive possibilities.) If Paul's Roman addressees, the gentiles-in-Christ, are former god-fearers—gentiles who as pagans had frequented Jewish synagogue communities—there's no reason to think that they would not still go to synagogue. Where else could they continue to hear the Bible, read aloud at least once a week in community? This gentile-ekklēsia-within-the-synagogue model could account both for the identity of Paul's addressees (they are ex-pagan gentiles) and for the issues that he treats (namely, relations between [non-Christian] Jews, such as would be found in the larger synagogue community, and baptized gentiles).

What resemblance does Paul's teaching have to that of Jesus? A number of themes in his letters cohere with those in the later gospels. This multiple attestation might be evidence that these themes can be traced back to Jesus' mission; see Fredriksen, *Jesus of Nazareth*, 74–154.

6. In Romans 9.4–5, Paul praises God for the privileges that he has conferred upon Israel. Paul writes (and I translate): "They are Israel, and to them belong the sonship, the glory of God's presence in the temple [Greek *doxa*], the covenants, the giving of the law, the temple's sacrificial cult [Greek *latreia*], and the promises; to them belong the patriarchs; and from their race, according to the flesh, is the messiah." The Greek word for "glory" sits on top of the Hebrew *kavod*, and refers specifically to the temple. So also *latreia*—translated in the Revised Standard Version as "worship"—means specifically "cult," and is therefore another nod toward Jerusalem and its temple. Standard English translations of these words blanket Paul's reference.

7. On the themes developed in Second Temple apocalyptic hope, see

Fredriksen, *From Jesus to Christ*, 73–93; on the eschatology of the first generation, see Allison, *Constructing Jesus*, 48–65; on Jerusalem in particular, see Sanders, *Jesus and Judaism*, 77–90.

8. E. P. Sanders, *The Historical Figure of Jesus*, 92, explains this two-word "code" for the Ten Commandments, noting that "these two words were used very widely by Greek-speaking Jews to summarize their religion." For John's mission, and his understanding of purity and the commandments, see Fredriksen, *Jesus of Nazareth*, 184–91.

9. This combination of purification and apocalyptic expectation also characterizes the sensibility of the Dead Sea Scrolls' community—which is not to say that John himself was an Essene. Sanders, *Judaism: Practice and Belief*, 367–79, gives a quick overview of that community's commitments.

10. On Matthew's "antitheses" (Mt 5.21–48), Sanders, *Historical Figure*, 210–12, comments,

> We ask . . . if in these passages whether Jesus opposes the law. The short answer is that he does not: rather, he requires a stricter code of practice. No one who observed the admonitions of Matthew 5 would transgress the law, and Jesus does not propose that any part of the Mosaic code should be repealed. . . . This section of Matthew has often been cited as showing Jesus' "opposition" to the law. But heightening the law is not opposing it.

Much of the material in the Sermon on the Mount is particular to Matthew; it is hard to say with security what might go back to Jesus himself. By considering such passages together with material in the Pauline epistles, however, we do get some traction on this slippery slope. It is clear from Galatians, for example, that the apostles still observe Jewish law, in this case about food (2.11–13). We can infer from this that Jesus did not teach against observing the law, or the controversy in Antioch would never have arisen.

11. Purity rules, exotic to us, were part and parcel of ancient religious culture both pagan and Jewish, because they were linked universally to protocols of sacrifice. For further discussion, and a reconstruction of Jesus' own practice of biblical purity, see Paula Fredriksen, "Did Jesus Oppose the Purity Laws?" and Fredriksen, *Jesus of Nazareth*, 197–207; a more recent, and exhaustive discussion is in Meier, *A Marginal Jew*, 4: 342–77, with copious bibliography. On Jewish purity practices more generally, see Jonathan Klawans, *Purity, Sacrifice, and the Temple*.

12. Identifications of Jesus as prophet *or* as messiah seesaw all throughout the Gospel of John: "This is indeed the prophet who is to come into the

world!" exclaims Jesus' audience (6.14). "Can it be that the authorities really know that this is the Christ?" (7.26). "Some of the people said, 'This is really the prophet,' while others said, 'This is the Christ,'" (7.40–41). "No prophet is to rise from Galilee" (7.52). "He is a prophet," asserts the blind man whom Jesus cures (9.17; cf. Lk 22.67, "If you are the Christ, then tell us!") By the time that the fourth evangelist writes, of course, much higher claim had been made for Jesus; perhaps, therefore, his identification as "prophet" as opposed to messiah dates from a much earlier stratum of tradition. On Jesus as *the* eschatological prophet, see Allison, *Constructing Jesus*, 270–74, with copious bibliography.

13. Josephus in *Antiquities* 18.63 characterizes Jesus as a worker of *para-doxa*, "startling deeds," perhaps a reference to the exorcisms and healings that the gospels credit Jesus with. On relationship of demons to disease, see further Meier, *A Marginal Jew*, 2:646–770. Popular pagan thought held similarly that gods or demons caused illness; see Dale B. Martin, *The Corinthian Body*, 153–59.

14. While clearly few Jews living in the Diaspora could make a pilgrimage to Jerusalem, nonpilgrims contributed to the cult, and thereby "benefited" from the sacrifices, through the voluntary "temple tax" of two drachmas (one-half shekel). Sanders, *Judaism: Practice and Belief*, 156, observes, "This is not a large sum: approximately two days' pay for a day laborer, a man at the bottom of the pay scale. That it was paid is one of the things about first-century Judaism that is most certain.". For a review and critique of the arguments that Jesus opposed Temple sacrifice, see Paula Fredriksen, "What You See Is What You Get."

15. For a narrative presentation of this reconstruction, see Sanders, *Historical Figure*, 250–52.

16. On the numerous divinities populating the ancient 'monotheist' cosmos, see, most recently, Paula Fredriksen, "Judaizing the Nations," esp. 236–37 on Jewish acknowledgment of—but not cult to—other pantheons. "After reading a certain document," announces the Spartan king to the Jewish high priest, "we have found that Jews and Lacedaemonians are one *genos*, and share a connection with Abraham" (1 Maccabees 12.21). This blood kinship (*suggeneia*) appears also in 2 Maccabees 5.9, and in Josephus' *Antiquities* 12.226. The "connection" goes back to Abraham, whose granddaughter, according to this Hellenistic Jewish story, married Heracles (*Antiquities* 1.240–41).

Ephesians, a letter by a later disciple writing in Paul's name, urges that the Christian himself combat the lower cosmic powers that Jews—and, later, Christians—often associated with Greco-Roman deities: "For our struggle is not against enemies of blood and flesh, but against the rulers, against the authorities, against the cosmic powers of this present darkness, against the spiritual forces of evil in the heavenly places" (Eph 6.12). Contra this interpretation of Paul's cosmic adversaries, see Allison, *Constructing Jesus*, 396–98.

17. Julia Severa, for example, a priestess of the imperial cult during the first century, built a synagogue in Acmonia for the community there; her generosity is recalled and acknowledged in a third-century inscription. On pagan benefaction to diaspora Jewish communities, see Lee I. Levine, *The Ancient Synagogue*, 111, 121, 479–83. A Jewish inscription from Aphrodisias, currently dated to the fourth and fifth centuries, indexes a mix of Jewish and gentile contributors to a community project according to their type of affiliation: it lists separately the Jews involved with the project, the converts ("proselytes"), and the fifty-four gentile god-fearers—pagans? Christians? we cannot tell—nine of whom are members of the town council. On this important inscription, see, most recently Angelos Chaniotis, "The Jews of Aphrodisias: New Evidence and Old Problems." For Christian complaints about Jews receiving pagans into synagogue communities, see Fredriksen, "Judaizing the Nations," 239–40.

18. Learned Greco-Roman ethnographies also routinely imputed sexual profligacy and homicide (indeed, cannibalism) to foreigners; Hellenistic Jews could thus avail themselves (as did the author of *Wisdom*) of both streams of abusive "othering." On polemical traditions of sexual accusation—which, as we will see in chapter 2, Christians could level against each other—see especially Jenny Knust, *Abandoned to Lust*; on ethnographies and interethnic abuse, see the magisterial study by Ben Isaac, *The Invention of Racism in Classical Antiquity*.

Rhetoric could heat up real life. The disastrous Jewish rebellion against Rome began in Caesarea, where pagan sacrifices, staged provocatively close to a synagogue, goaded local Jews to riot and eventually led the country into open rebellion (*Jewish War* 2.285–88). And during the mysterious uprising of the Jews of Cyprus and Cyrene in the years between the first Judaean revolt (66–73 CE) and the last (132–35 CE, under Bar Kokhba), the bloodshed was accompanied by the deliberate desecration and destruction of pagan temples. For the most part, though, rhetoric did remain rhetoric. And, of course, the subjects presented in such writings were not "real people" but "rhetorical people," a constructed antitype that revealed a reverse image of the idealized self. Such rhetoric offers not description but caricature. *Wisdom's* rhetorical gentiles were the reverse image of the idealized Jew.

19. But what about eating meat that had been sacrificed to idols: does that not constitute worshiping the gods? On this point Paul is surprisingly flexible. People who partake in a sacrificial meal, he says, repeating a Mediterranean commonplace, become coparticipants not only with each other but also with the divinity being so honored: true of the "people of Israel," who thereby become "partners in [God's] altar"; true of pagans who, though they think that they are worshiping gods, are actually sacrificing to lesser and malevolent powers, *daimones*, "demons." "I do not want you to be partners with demons," Paul tells his community in Corinth. "You cannot drink the cup of the Lord and the cup of demons. You cannot partake of the table of the Lord and the table of demons" (1 Cor 10.18–21). So: no participation in public ritual. What about the meat in the marketplace? "Eat whatever is sold in the meat market without raising any question on the grounds of conscience," he advises. What about eating dinner at a pagan's house? "Eat whatever is set before you without raising any question on the ground of conscience." Idols are nugatory, the gods that they represent are lowly powers, the produce of the earth is the Lord's—all reasons, says Paul, to go ahead and eat (10.25–27. For all we know, what Paul repeats here is the modus vivendi of many diaspora Jews). The only reason not to eat is if a fellow Christian hesitates out of scruple. ("But if someone says to you, 'This has been offered in sacrifice,' then do not eat it, out of consideration for the one who informed you, and for the sake of conscience—not yours, but his"; 10.28–29.) He makes the same point, more succinctly, in Romans 14.20: "Do not, for the sake of food, destroy the work of God."

20. In antiquity, *cult* was an ethnic designation, and *ethnicity* was a cult designation. What we think of as "conversion" meant, in antiquity, assuming the ancestral practices of another group, tantamount to changing ethnicity. Pagans who complain about fellow pagans' "becoming" Jews present this as a choice between "Roman custom" and "the customs of the Jews."

The problem with refusing to honor one's own gods—a consequence of "conversion" to Judaism—was that lack of cult made gods angry, and angry gods might subvert the well-being of the entire larger pagan community. This was a real concern and a perceived danger. As Robin Lane Fox, *Pagans and Christians*, 39, notes,

> From Britain to Syria, pagan cults aimed to honor the gods and avert the misfortunes which might result from the gods' own anger at their neglect. Any account of pagan worship which minimizes the gods' uncertain anger and mortals' fear of it is an empty account.

Paul's people, whom he attempts to render ex-pagan pagans, would be perceived by their larger urban community to present a similar danger.

21. For a review of both inclusive and exclusive passages, see Paula Fredriksen, "Judaism, the Circumcision of Gentiles, and Apocalyptic Hope," 543–48, with references; on the ways that this conviction about eschatological gentiles informs the early mission, see Fredriksen, *Jesus of Nazareth*, 125–37 (Paul) and 261–66 (the original disciples). "There simply was no unified view whatsoever on the religious status of non-Jews, either now or in the future. The range of diversity is striking," notes Terry Donaldson, *Judaism and Gentiles*, 512. On the gentiles' participation in Israel's eschatological salvation, see Donaldson, *Judaism and Gentiles*, 499–507.

22. The spirit, conferred on Paul's gentiles through baptism, puts them in a special state not only morally but cosmically. This is so because of Paul's apocalyptic opposition of *pneuma* (spirit) and *sarx* (flesh). As Martin, *Corinthian Body*, 172–73 notes,

> Sarx and pneuma constitute a radical dualism in Paul's ethical cosmos. . . . the overwhelming bulk of his references to sarx place it in the category of "this world" in its opposition to the plan of God. . . . Paul also speaks of Pneuma and Sarx as anthropomorphic or hypostatized powers of the cosmos. Pneuma is the power that enables sarx to live, although it is also in continual battle with it. . . . They wage constant warfare in the cosmos at large, a war that is fought out on a small scale in the bodies of women and men.

23. On this last point, see the now classic essay by Krister Stendahl, "Paul and the Introspective Conscience of the West"; on the ways that Augustine's later reading of this difficult passage bequeaths the "autobiographical" interpretation to later Western Christian tradition, see Paula Fredriksen, "Paul and Augustine: Conversion Narratives, Orthodox Traditions, and the Retrospective Self." On role-playing as a technique of ancient rhetoric, especially as that effects how we understand the "I" of Romans 7, see Stanley Stowers, *A Rereading of Romans*, 251–84. As Stowers notes, some of the set speeches in classical drama echo exactly the ideas that Paul presents in Romans 7.

24. "What human beings have in common with heavenly bodies is, in Paul's system, incorporation as a 'pneumatic body'—that is, a body composed only of pneuma, with sarx and psyche having been sloughed off along the way," notes Martin, who observes also that the contrast between pneuma/

spirit and sarx/flesh is not one of immaterial/material: "Neither Paul nor most of the philosophers of his day considered celestial bodies 'immaterial' in our sense of the term." Martin, *Corinthian Body*, 126, 127; for Martin's whole discussion of astral body in antiquity, see 117–29. The very visibility of celestial powers, of course, was evidence of their embodiment. The *soma pneumatikon*, the risen spiritual body of the (Pauline) redeemed Christian, will have sloughed off flesh and soul and retained only its pneuma, "a stuff of a thinner, higher nature." Martin, *Corinthian Body*, 128.

25. On patterns of pollution and sacrifice cleansing the sancta of the temple, see Jacob Milgrom, *Leviticus 1–16*, 254–58. Klawans, *Impurity and Sin in Ancient Judaism*, 3–20, offers a succinct review of various scholarly reconstructions. Stowers, *A Rereading of Romans*, 206–13, suggests that *hilasterion*, translated "expiation" in the Revised Standard Version, might be better understood as "act of reconciliation" in a nonsacrificial sense. He also observes that ancient sacrifice emphasized not the *death* of the animal (as Christian understandings of Jesus' death as a sacrifice tend to do) but the ritualized disorganization and reorganization of the animal's body: "Sacrifice is not about death or ritual killing" (207).

26. "I have written to you very boldly," Paul says toward the end of Romans (and I translate), "because of the grace given to me by God to be Jesus Christ's temple assistant [RSV: "minister"] for the gentiles, sacrificing God's good news [RSV: "in priestly service to gospel"], so that the offering that is the gentiles may be acceptable, made holy by the holy spirit" (Rm 15.15–16). For a longer discussion of this interpretation, see Fredriksen, "Judaizing the Nations," 244–49.

27. Given antiquity's identification of ethnicity and what we think of as "religion," the idea of a "mission" to change pagans into Jews is counterintuitive; and, in fact, we have no evidence of such missions *except* for this unknown group of Paul's Christian competitors in Galatians. See further Fredriksen, "Judaizing the Nations," 242–44; also Fredriksen, "Judaism, the Circumcision of Gentiles, and Apocalyptic Hope"; and Martin Goodman, *Mission or Conversion*.

28. A chestnut of older New Testament scholarship on Paul was the principle that Paul—and, some said, Jesus—urged that followers abandon Jewish "ritual" law and keep only the "ethical" law. These categories are anachronistic, and deeply nonnative to the tradition that they supposedly describe. More to the point, Paul's premier demand—no idol worship!—is specifically about right and wrong "ritual" behavior.

29. "All Israel," by Paul's lifetime, had been missing since shortly after

722 BCE when the Assyrians, conquering the Israelite northern kingdom (corresponding to present-day Galilee), dispersed the ten "lost" tribes within their own territories—which is to say, among "the gentiles." Does Paul's eschatological ingathering of the "full number" of the gentiles mean, then, that these tribes, long dispersed among the gentiles, are the subjects of salvation? In other words, does saving "*all* Israel," including these ten missing tribes, require the *pleroma* of the gentiles? For this intriguing argument, see Jason Staples, "What Do the Gentiles Have to Do with 'All Israel'?"

30. In the words of Krister Stendahl, *Final Account*, 7, "When I teach this, many Christian theologians say, 'You teach two ways of salvation, one for Jews and one for Christians.' But I do no such thing. I would just call this arrangement God's traffic plan. And Paul called it a mystery."

Chapter 2. Flesh and the Devil: Sin in the Second Century

1. For Paul's many references to other gods in his letters, see James Dunn, *The Theology of the Apostle Paul*, 33–38. Beyond this geocentric model of the universe, the zodiac itself was an ecumenical road map of reality, invoked in pagan, Jewish, and Christian art and architecture. Valentinian Christians, according to Clement of Alexandria, *Excerpts from Theodotos* XXV, 1, associated the twelve apostles with "the twelve signs of the zodiac. For just as birth is regulated by them [that is, by the astral deities], so is *re*birth directed by the apostles."

2. Matter altered, bodies became finer as they ascended in the cosmic order. Paul pays homage to this way of understanding body in 1 Corinthians 15.39–42:

> For not all flesh is alike, but there is one kind for men, another for animals, another for birds, another for fish. There are celestial bodies and there are terrestrial bodies; but the glory of the celestial is one, and the glory of the terrestrial is another. There is one glory of the sun, and another glory of the moon, and another glory of the stars; for star differs from star in glory. So it is with the resurrection of the dead. What is sown is perishable, what is raised is imperishable. . . . It is sown a physical body, it is raised a *soma pneumatikon*, a spiritual body.

Note: Paul is not a Platonist. Platonists held that spirit was another order of being, utterly immaterial. Paul's philosophical orientation is Stoic: the "spiritual body" is made out of very fine matter, but it is still matter—as is spirit (*pneuma*) itself. On Paul's underlying Stoic presuppositions, see Martin, *Corinthian Body*; and most recently, Troels Engberg-Pedersen, *Cosmology and Self in the Apostle Paul: The Material Spirit*. Engberg-Pedersen notes that while Paul's cosmology is Stoic-materialist, his *theology* is not: "Paul's God was just the Jewish God" (61), meaning that Paul did not conceive God as material, too.

Hulē qua formless matter functioned as the extreme notional counterpoint to *ho theos*, the transcendent high god of more Platonic forms of theology: in reality, matter was encountered only with form. The idea firewalls the high god's radical stability and unchangingness. Positing hyle allowed ancients to posit as well the coeternal nature of the cosmos, which—since this substratum also always existed—was likewise necessary to protect God from change. This principle was one of the "common conceptions to which all men agree as soon as they are asked," writes Sallustius, a fourth-century pagan Neoplatonist, in his treatise *On the Gods and the Cosmos*: "For instance, that all God is good, free from passion, free from change" (I). As he notes later, regarding the universe, "The cosmos must of necessity be indestructible and uncreated. . . . Since the cosmos exists by the goodness of God it follows that God must *always* be good and the cosmos always exit, just as light coexists with the Sun and with fire, and shadow coexists with body" (VII). Later Christian theologians would use the same language to describe how the Son was always coeternal with the Father.

Philosophically sophisticated biblical commentators easily saw such hyle in the opening verses of Genesis LXX, where the world "was without form and void." Philo of Alexandria takes this language to imply preexistent matter—for example, in *Life of Moses* 2.267. Later Christian theologians went back and forth on the issue: did preexistent matter imply some limit on God? Why should he be necessarily dependent on anything? If God were all good, then was not hyle "bad," in which case, why would God have organized it and pronounced the creation based upon it "good"?

Creation ex nihilo ultimately carried the day, to the point that Origen of Alexandria, in the third century, could muse, "Regarding this *hulē*, which is so great and wonderful as to be sufficient for all the bodies in the world, which God willed to exist . . . I cannot understand how so many distinguished men have supposed it to be uncreated" (*On First Principles* II. i, 4). For a very clear discussion of the Christian arguments about hyle's status, see Henry Chadwick, *Early Christian Thought and the Classical Tradition*, 46–48 and notes.

3. The famous Oenoanda inscription presents Apollo speaking of this highest deity while referring to himself and to the other lower gods as angels: "Born of itself, without a mother, unshakable, not contained in a name, known by many names, dwelling in fire, this is God. We, his *angeloi* [messengers] are a small part of God . . ." For more on this hexameter hymn and the pagan cult of the highest god, see Stephen Mitchell, "The Cult of Theos Hypsistos between Pagans, Jews, and Christians"; the inscription is given in full on 82. Hellenistic Judaism employed many divine mediating figures to bridge the gap between God and the world: various angels especially, but also God's Sophia ("Wisdom") and his word ("Logos"); two books by Alan Segal, *Paul the Convert* and *Two Powers in Heaven*, give good orientations in the relevant material. Justin Martyr was comfortable referring to Christ as God's *angelos* (*Trypho* 56, 59). Both the imagined architecture of the universe and the definition of the high god called into being multiple divine intermediaries; as Sallustius observed, "The further removed the First God is from our nature, the more powers [Greek *dunameis*] there must be between us and him. For all things that are very far apart have many intermediate points between them" (*On the Gods and the Cosmos* XIII).

Demons (*daimones*), as noted above, originally served as the pagan word for "lower divinities," which could be either morally good or morally not so good. Despite Paul's—and later Christian theology's—unequivocal denunciation of demons as evil, they retained a certain moral ambiguity, haunting the graves of martyrs, giving true prophecies, presiding over healings, and so on; see David Frankfurter, "Where the Spirits Dwell: Possession, Christianization, and Saints' Shrines in Late Antiquity."

4. Modern monotheism posits that only one god exists; ancient monotheism—sometimes referred to as "henotheism"—conjectured one supreme god amid other, lower gods. But those ancient populations habitually spoken of as "monotheist"—namely, Jews and Christians—clearly lived in the same god-congested universe as their pagan contemporaries. For that reason, academic vocabulary currently distinguishes between "ancient" and "modern" monotheism, and likewise refers to "pagan monotheism." Not all pagans were (ancient) monotheists, but many monotheists were pagans. Besides the essays collected in Polymnia Athanassiadi and Michael Frede, eds., *Pagan Monotheism*, see also Stephen Mitchell and Peter van Nuffelen, eds., *One God*. On the confusions and anachronisms occasioned by the use of the word "monotheist" for ancient Jews and Christians, see Paula Fredriksen, "Mandatory Retirement: Ideas in the Study of Ancient Christianity Whose Time to Go Has Come."

5. From the perspective of Roman-era Stoicism, Martin, *Corinthian Body*, 117–20, provides a wonderfully clear orientation in ancient anthropology, and in the ways that humans, shedding flesh, become stars after death.

6. Ancient rhetoricians were trained not so much in how to interpret a text as in how to conduct an *argument* about how to interpret a text. The goal was not to find the "true interpretation" of a text (texts were ambiguous, and could hold many meanings) but to persuade those listening that one's opponent was completely wrong, and that one's own interpretation was the only possible right one. Students were made to master a whole range of traditional arguments together with their coordinating counterarguments, and rhetorical imagination and agility were measured by the successful application of these topoi. Those trained in rhetoric imagined, practiced, and performed interpretive argument as an *agōn*, a trial or contest or competition. For a pellucid discussion of these techniques and a lively tour through one famous rhetorical/theological contest, see especially Margaret M. Mitchell, "Patristic Rhetoric on Allegory: Origen and Eustasthius Put 1 Samuel 28 on Trial."

7. "Peter" may have been objecting to nonapocalyptic readings of the Apostle; in this same letter, he criticizes other Christians who "scoff," saying, "Where is the promise of [Christ's second] Coming? For ever since the fathers fell asleep, all things have continued as they were since the beginning of creation" (2 Pt 3.4. The author responds to this question by presenting an apocalyptic calculus that explains why things are taking such a long time; see n. 29, below.

8. That gods were defeated when their people were was an extension of the normal identification of ethnic groups with their particular pantheons. The first Jewish revolt happened to coincide with the abrupt ending of the Julio-Claudian dynasty in the person of the emperor Nero: in the confusion of the "year of the four emperors," when military strongmen contested for the purple, Jews benefited from the empire's distraction. Good luck, bad luck: it was Vespasian, the general charged with suppressing the Jewish revolt, who succeeded Nero, and from that point on, the prestige of the new dynasty was linked to glorifying the victory over the Jews.

The Jews' defeat in 70 and again in 135 caused a problem for those Christians who insisted that their god was the deity of the Jewish scriptures. Judea "would never have been put beneath your scepter," writes Tertullian, "if not for that last and crowning offense against God in rejecting and crucifying Christ" (1 *Apology* 26). "The lonely and miserable nationality of the Jews worshipped one God, and one peculiar to itself," runs another apology, voicing a pagan perspective, "and he has so little force or power, that he is enslaved, with his own special nation, to the Roman deities"; Minucius Felix, *Octavius* 10.4.

9. Thus the Valentinian Ptolemy, *Letter to Flora* VII, 7–8: "The nature of the ungenerated Father of All is incorruption and self-existent, simple, and homogeneous light. . . . One . . . ungenerated, incorruptible, and good." And Justin: "That which always maintains the same nature, and in the same manner, and is the cause of all other things—that, indeed, is God" (*Trypho* 3). We cannot quote Marcion—no text of his exists—but his description of the high god is embedded in Tertullian's first book against him, *Against Marcion*, 1. For an analysis of Tertullian's quarrel with Marcion as specifically over theology—"the nature of God and the criteria for understanding it"—see Judith Lieu, "'As Much My Apostle as Christ Is Mine'." In the late fourth century, the Manichaean teacher Faustus identified the belief that a single principle stands as source of cosmos as an idea held in common by pagans, Jews, and catholics; see Augustine, *Against Faustus* 20.4.

10. For a while, all three of these independent Christian theologians lived and taught in Rome. David Brakke, *The Gnostics*, 92, notes that "the issues that Gnostic teachings raised—the identity of the God of Israel, the status of the Jewish scriptures, acquaintance with the ultimate God—figure prominently in the work of early Roman Christian teachers."

11. This description of so-called Gnostic sexual antinomianism paraphrases that found in Henry Chadwick, *The Early Church*, 34–41; Chadwick's is still a classroom standard. Similarly, Hans Jonas, *The Gnostic Religion*, 46, speculates about Gnostic asceticism and "libertinism" as the two extremes made possible by their "hostility toward the world and contempt for all mundane ties. . . . This antinomian libertinism exhibits more forcefully than the ascetic version the *nihilistic* element contained in gnostic acosmism." Kurt Rudolph gives a review of heresiological witnesses and the modern history of research, in *Gnosis*, 9–30; see also the convenient compendium in Werner Foerster, *Gnosis: A Selection of Gnostic Texts*, vol. 1. Against using the term *Gnosticism* at all, see Karen King, *What Is Gnosticism?*; for an argument for the use of the term—but distinguishing Valentinians from Gnostic Christians—see Brakke, *Gnostics*. Finally, Michel Desjardins, *Sin in Valentinianism*, 19–66, gives a very useful overview of those documents found in the Nag Hammadi Library that may be identified as Valentinian.

12. There are two standard translations: the older is James M. Robinson, ed., *The Nag Hammadi Library*; the newer is Bentley Layton, ed., *The Gnostic Scriptures*. For Marcion, the single best source for reconstructing his teachings comes from the lengthy work of his nemesis, Tertullian, *Against Marcion*.

As Brakke, *Gnostics*, 96, notes, "Marcion's teachings represent a strikingly streamlined alternative to the Gnostic myth, while speaking to some of the same concerns." On Marcion's fundamental importance to understanding second-century Christianity, see John Marshall, "Misunderstanding the New Paul: Marcion's Transformation of the *Sonderzeit* Paul."

13. Modern scholarship still looks back to Adolf von Harnack's 1924 study for the broad outlines of our understanding of Marcion, *Marcion: the Gospel of the Alien God*; valuable is Judith Lieu's discussion in *Image and Reality*, 261–70. For recent challenges to this older orthodoxy, see Sebastian Moll, *The Arch-Heretic Marcion*, and Judith Lieu, "'As Much My Apostle as Christ Is Mine'." Marcion compiled the *Antitheses*, which laid out contrasting teachings between the LXX and Paul. His gathering together of a version of Luke's gospel together with ten Pauline letters (Galatians, 1 and 2 Corinthians, Romans, 1 and 2 Thessalonians, Ephesians [called Laodiceans], Colossians, Philippians, and Philemon), which he presented as the sole scriptures for the Christian, spurred his opponents to conceive a broader New Testament canon.

14. On the problems with such terms as *orthodoxy, proto-orthodoxy, heresy*, and the like for constructing a model for understanding second- through fourth-century Christianity that does not simply repeat the language of the winners, see Brakke, *Gnostics*, 1–28, "Imagining 'Gnosticism' and Early Christianities." Brakke notes that "discovering what Valentinus taught is a formidable task, and scholars disagree about many important points," including "how much we can use Valentinus' followers, especially Ptolemy, to reconstruct his thought" (100).

15. See Jenny Knust, *Abandoned to Lust*, for a wonderful tour through the tangle of hostile rhetoric and sexual accusations that shape pagan discourse and Jewish and intra-Christian polemic; see especially p. 130 for the ways that modern scholars uncritically repeat such rhetoric as if it were historical description. Imputations of sexual profligacy regularly appear together with accusations of cannibalism in the learned descriptions of foreign others in classical ethnographies; on which see Isaac, *Invention of Racism*, s.v. "cannibalism." Pagans accused Christians of such behaviors, and Christians accused other Christians of the same (hence Justin's dark allusion to the "nefarious and impious rites" of Valentinians and Marcionites, *Trypho* 35; so also 1 *Apology* 26).

16. I blend translations here from Werner Foerster, *Gnosis: A Selection of Gnostic Texts*, 2:57, and from Layton, *The Gnostic Scriptures*, as cited in Brakke, *Gnostics*, 102. Brakke continues,

> The sermon *The Gospel of Truth* includes an extensive meditation on the relationship between the Son and the Father. . . . Here the crucifixion, as the moment when *gnosis* of God becomes possible, looks backward to the Fall in Eden and forward to the Christian Eucharist. By eating the body of Christ, Christians participate in the crucifixion of Christ and gain knowledge of God and of themselves, for God is within them as the inconceivable origin of all that truly is. In contrast to the Eden story, this knowledge brings joy and life, not regret and ruin.

Sin, then, is due to ignorance of the Father, "but sin itself remains wrong action, that is, an action not in accord with the Father's will," Michel Desjardins, *Sin in Valentinianism*, 80.

17. On the importance of self-knowledge as revelation in Valentinus, and the ways that this Platonic theme fuses with his Christian vision, see Simone Pétrement, *A Separate God*, 371–78.

18. Sophia's saga—breaking off from her consort, afflicted by a desire that she cannot assuage, driven on by passion—draws surprisingly on another source, Greek medical science. According to some ancient gynecologists, lack of sexual intercourse can cause the womb/*hystera* to dry out and thereby become light, so that it wanders into the upper parts of the body. This causes a condition known as "hysterical suffocation," or *hysteriké pniz*, characterized by dissociation, sleepiness, pain, and disorder. By breaking off from her consort, Sophia, driven by unrequited passion, replicates this condition; and so she wanders, disoriented and driven, into the upper Pleroma where she does not belong. Plato had also referred to the wandering womb (*Timaeus* 91c). For more, see Paula Fredriksen, "Hysteria and the Gnostic Myths of Creation."

19. The *Excerpts of Theodotos* are preserved in Clement of Alexandria's baggy work, *Miscellanies*. Elsewhere, Clement quotes Valentinus as speaking of "evil spirits" that afflict the human heart, dwelling in it and treating it abusively "by means of unseemly desires." The true source of the evil desires, which are sinful, is these spirits, not the afflicted person. But, teaches Clement, through the One,

> whose manifestation through the Son gives confidence . . . it is possible for the heart to become pure, when every evil spirit is banished. . . . The heart, so long as it is not cared for, is unclean and the abode of many demons. But when the Father, who alone is good, visits it, it is sanctified and becomes bright with light; and he who has such a heart will be proclaimed blessed, for he will see God (Mt 5.8). (*Miscellanies* 2.20)

20. I quote Ernest Evans's preface to the critical edition of Tertullian's work, *Against Marcion*, 1.14. On the grudging acknowledgment of the Marcionites' ethic of martyrdom, see Eusebius, *A History of the Church*, 5.16.20.

21. As Marshall, "Misunderstanding the New Paul," notes, p. 6:

> Paul's rhetorical strategy in Romans seems to have been a failure in the sense that his later readers give no evidence of grasping the complex interplay of voices with which Paul constructs his argument. It is as if Paul delights in leading his readers at high speed toward a logical precipice, stepping aside and interjecting *me genoito* with the expectation that they will not sail over the precipice but merely experience a pedagogically productive whiplash. In practice, it seems that they usually sailed over the precipice.

I thank John Marshall for sharing a prepublication version of his essay with me.

22. This construal of Marcion is indebted to Marshall's argument in "Misunderstanding the New Paul"; cf. (to my regret) Paula Fredriksen, *Augustine and the Jews*, 226.

23. While heresiologists report that Valentinians, on account of this schema, left no scope for free will, the documents found at the Nag Hammadi Library imply otherwise. There, *psuchikoi* and *pneumatikoi* together compose the community; psychics receive instruction, and are empowered to resist evil by receiving baptism. Free will was the lynchpin of Greek moral philosophy, definitive of the rational being. To claim that a group disputed free will and thought that moral attainment occurred through nature and not through effort was tantamount to saying that first, they did not believe in or, therefore, practice virtue, and thus were bad people; and second, that they fundamentally misunderstood rationality, and hence were bad philosophers; cf. Justin, *Trypho* 141 on the free will of men and of angels.

24. Justin's identity as a philosopher is very important to him: he opens his dialogue by emphasizing it (*Trypho* 1). Justin feels that his philosophy (that is, his version of Christianity) is superior to other philosophies because it transforms the unlettered—even women!—into sober, self-disciplined people (2 *Apology* 2, 9).

25. "God . . . committed the care of men and of all things to angels whom he appointed over them. But the angels transgressed this appointment, and were captivated by the love of women, and begat children who are called demons" (2 *Apology* 5); cf. *Trypho* 79. These angels and their demonic progeny

then led humanity astray by introducing magic, sacrilegious sacrifices, sowing murder and adulteries among men. For further analysis of the multiple uses that Justin puts these demons to, see Annette Reed, "The Trickery of the Fallen Angels."

26. These god-fearers are voluntary, pagan Judaizers; see p. 25.

27. Earlier speeches by "Peter" prepare the reader for this accusation. When speaking to Jerusalem's Jews—and even to Jewish pilgrims who had not been in the city when Jesus was killed (Acts 2.9–11)—Peter indicts his hearers. He continues: "This man [Jesus], handed over to you according to the definite plan and foreknowledge of God, *you crucified and killed* by the hands of those outside the Law" (2.23). *"Let the entire house of Israel know* with certainty that God has made him both Lord and Messiah, this *Jesus whom you crucified"* (2.36). "You rejected the Holy and Righteous One . . . *you killed the Author of life,* whom God raised from the dead" (3.15). "The God of our ancestors raised up *Jesus, whom you killed by hanging him on a tree.* God exalted him at his right hand as leader and savior that he might give repentance to Israel and forgiveness of sins" (5.30–31). Whatever the myriad other sins Israel has to repent for, this huge transgression ranks foremost. The death of Jesus is *the* sin for which Jews must repent. But how? According to Luke, in one way only, by being baptized into the new community: "Repent and be baptized every one of you in the name of Jesus Christ, so that your sins may be forgiven" (2.38).

Jewish responsibility for the death of Jesus is a prominent theme in the gospels, introduced and developed especially through the device of the Passion predictions, embellished narratively once Jesus reaches Jerusalem for the final time, and eventually when he stands before Pilate. As the Passion narratives develop, Roman responsibility diminishes as Pilate's reluctance grows. In the Gospel of John, Jesus has to persuade Pilate to get on with the execution (19.11). See Paula Fredriksen, *Jesus to Christ,* 107–11, 115–22.

28. The full passage runs:

> In like manner as Jesus Christ our savior, having been made flesh by the logos of God, had both flesh and blood for our salvation, so likewise we have been taught that the food which is blessed by the prayer of his word, and from which our blood and flesh are nourished by transformation, is the flesh and blood of that Jesus who was made flesh. (1 *Apology* 66)

The language resonates with the image of sacrifice. I thank my colleague Jenny Knust for helping me think through Justin's imagery here.

29. Justin's own passage invokes some of the scriptural building blocks of this patristic tradition of millenarian calculations: the six days of Creation (Gen 1); the thousand-year reign of the saints (Rv 20.4–5); and "a thousand years is as a day in the sight of the Lord" (Ps 90.4, cited already in 2 Pt 3.8 to account for the delay of the End: God was not late, he only *seemed* late.) These combined to form the foundation for calculations of the "cosmic week," or the six ages of the world. At the end of the sixth "day" or age, the year 6000 since the world's foundation, Christ would return in glory to establish his saints' reign, the millennial Sabbath rest. To know the time of the End, one then had to calculate the age of the world. In the Western tradition of millenarian calculation, the year 6000 since the creation fell variously between the years 400 to 500 CE. This millenarian tradition cohered effortlessly with incarnationalist Christology and with the belief in the physical resurrection. In *City of God* Augustine had to do some very fancy exegesis in order to maintain both that the physical body would be raised and that the eschatological kingdom would come not on earth but in heaven; see p. 128; see also the article "Apocalypticism," in Allan Fitzgerald, ed., *Augustine through the Ages: An Encyclopedia*, 49–53; and Fredriksen, "Apocalypse and Redemption."

Chapter 3. A Rivalry of Genius: Sin and Its
Consequences in Origen and Augustine

I purloin this chapter title from the learned essay with the same title by my friend and colleague Marc Hirshman.

1. The details of Origen's enormous corpus of work are given in Johannes Quasten, *Patrology* 2:43–75; for Augustine, see Quasten, *Patrology* 4:355–403. The print calculation of Augustine's output comes from James J. O'Donnell, *Augustine: A New Biography*, 136.

2. Written in Alexandria circa 232, this masterwork fell victim to the posthumous controversy that surrounded Origen's legacy in the centuries after his death. As a result, the text itself is in tatters: The scientific edition in *Greichischen Christlichen Shriftsteller* is a pastiche of various Greek fragments, texts from the Second Council of Constantinople anathematizing Origen in 553, and an early fifth-century Latin targum by Rufinus composed with an eye toward protecting Origen from the objections and accusations that his work already attracted.

3. As Origen says,

> The scriptures . . . have not only that meaning which is obvious, but also another which is hidden from the majority of readers. For the contents of scripture are the outward forms of certain mysteries and the images of divine things. On this point the entire church is unanimous, that while the whole law is spiritual, the inspired meaning is not recognized by all, but only by those who are gifted with the grace of the Holy Spirit in the word of wisdom and knowledge. (I. praef., 8)

"The Word of God has arranged for certain stumbling-blocks and hindrances and impossibilities to be inserted in the midst of the law and the history" (IV. ii, 9) so that the alert reader is cued to a deeper meaning. One such, Origen observes, is the law's prohibition to eat vultures. "Clearly irrational," he notes, "as no one even in the worst famine was ever driven by want to the extremity of eating these creatures!" (IV. iii, 2). The prohibition, accordingly, must have other than a literal meaning. Ilaria Ramelli explores Origen's debts and contributions to the philosophical discussion of allegory in part 3 of "The Philosophical Stance of Allegory."

4. Origen here attempts to square the circle of having a changeless god, the source of everything else, relate to a changeful and material universe. One way was to have *hulē* coeternal with the high god, and *cosmos*—the ordered universe—as a kind of "instantaneous" coeternal precipitate that could then be managed by lower deities. This is the tack taken by the Neoplatonist Sallustius in his fourth-century pagan "catechism" *On the Gods and the Cosmos.* Origen's first cosmos, spiritual and unchanging, can be eternally produced by the One since, before matter, there is no time. The One also eternally produces the Son and the Holy Spirit as incorporeal refractions of himself: there was never a "time" when the Father was without Son, and so on. When matter is created, it is done through the Logos, and not directly "by" the high god.

Augustine will square this circle similarly by dwelling on the "cognitive" differences between humans in time and God eternally outside of time; see p. 118.

5. How many of these spiritual, rational beings did God "create"? Origen argues that there must have been a specific number, because logically not even God can contain the infinite (IV. iv, 8). These creatures' free will is what makes them morally responsible for their choices; without that autonomy, God could not be just, whether in disciplining or in rewarding.

6. Origen describes how all but one of these rational beings wavered in its affectionate concentration on their maker. That one more constant being, through the free exercise of its own will, loved God with such ardor that it

fused with its "object," the Logos (II. vi, 3): the soul of Jesus thus merged with the godhead of Christ. All the other rational beings slipped away—some, like Satan, to the maximum degree imaginable. The "soul" represented by these rational beings in turn functions as the mean term between "spirit" and "flesh": soul enables spirit to be attached to fleshly body. Origen's description of the precosmic history of Jesus' soul is thus an antidocetic argument that looks ahead to the Son's incarnation in time: had Jesus' soul in the time before time *not* adhered in this way to God, Christ could not have truly assumed flesh.

7. Origen goes into some detail on matter as hyle: for him, it is formless in and of itself, but *not* eternal (II. i, 3–4)—a distinction with much difference.

8. Origen is forthright about the status of his ideas: this is not doctrine but informed speculation. Concluding his discussion on "the end of all things," he writes, "Each of our readers must judge for himself, with all care and diligence, whether one [of his ideas about the End] may be approved and adopted" (II. iii, 7).

9. Origen's argument about God's justice is motivated in part to protect God—and the biblical language of election—from any imputation of arbitrariness. He therefore also takes aim against the Valentinians and Marcionites who claim (Origen says) that believers are saved "by nature" (III. i, 8–9).

10. Origen urges that the soul's preexistence is necessary to make moral sense of God's choice of Jacob over Esau:

> Now with regard to man, how could it be possible that the soul of him who "supplanted his brother in the womb," that is, Jacob, was formed at the same time as his body? . . . Otherwise it would appear that God fills some men with the Holy Spirit regardless of the justice of their merits and sanctifies them when they have dome nothing to deserve it. And if that were so, how should we avoid the difficulty expressed in that passage in which it is said, "Is there unrighteousness with God? God forbid (Rm 9.14)!" (I. vii, 4)

On the redemption of celestial rational beings, see Alan Scott, *Origen and the Life of the Stars*.

11. Origen writes,

> We have mentioned all these instances with the object of showing that the aim of the divine power which bestowed on us the holy scriptures is not that we should accept only what is found in the letter; for occasionally the records taken in a literal sense are not true, but actually

absurd and impossible, and even with the history that actually happened and in the legislation that is in its literal sense useful there are other matters interwoven. (IV. 3, 4)

12. The one "fact" about Origen that even people who have not read him seem to know is that he supposedly castrated himself, following too literally the injunction in Matthew's gospel that some men make themselves eunuchs for the sake of the kingdom of heaven (Mt 19.12). This tradition appears in Eusebius, *Ecclesiastical History*, 6.8. Epiphanius, in *Panarion* 64.3,11–12, attributes Origen's remarkable self-control to his use of drugs. See the discussion in Chadwick, *Early Christian Thought*, 67ff.

13. Augustine worked on the twenty-two books of the *City of God* off and on from 413 to 428; along with his lengthy refutation in thirty-three books of Latin Manichaeism, *Against Faustus*, he referred to *City* as a "magnum opus." If the whole cosmos, both eternal and embodied, provided Origen with his canvas for *On First Principles*, then all of history, from the fall of the angels to the triumph of heaven—with long passages in between reviewing the history of Rome and of Israel—provided Augustine with his.

14. Augustine felt the lack of the Greek commentaries most acutely, and asked Jerome to stop bothering with his biblical translations and to concentrate instead on patristic writings, most especially Origen's (*ep.* 28.2, 2). Two excellent—and very different—biographies present Augustine's character, intellectual and political, in the round: Peter Brown, *Augustine of Hippo*; and James O'Donnell, *Augustine: A New Biography*. On Augustine's knowledge of Greek, O'Donnell expends one word: "Pathetic" (126).

15. These issues swirled among theologians in the generations following Origen. The Pelagian controversy—fought over the issue of free will and Augustine's doctrine of original sin—was in many ways the specifically Latin phase of this protracted response to Origen's work; see especially Elizabeth A. Clark, *The Origenist Controversy*.

16. Adam appears at a crucial turning point in a public debate that Augustine conducted with an old Manichaean colleague of his, Fortunatus, when Augustine sought to defend the idea divine justice together with a catholic reading of Paul's letters (*Against Fortunatus* 22); in the year following that debate, in 393, he would start and leave off his first attempt to interpret Genesis "historically" in the *Unfinished Literal Commentary on Genesis*.

17. The figure of Adam continued to evolve in the works on Paul that Augustine produced in the years immediately preceding the appearance of the *Confessions*, between 394 and 397. For this particular construal of "human

nature," see 66.1–2, 6 of *Eighty-three Different Questions*, commenting again on Romans; see also the discussion in Paula Fredriksen, *Augustine and the Jews*, 155–72 and notes.

18. Augustine works this out, again considering Romans 9–11, in his *Response to Simplicianus*; see the discussion in Fredriksen, *Augustine and the Jews*, 172-82. His later teaching on original sin represents a refinement of this idea, stated concisely in *City of God*:

> The whole human race was in the first man, and it [death] was to pass from him through the woman into his progeny, when the married pair received the divine sentence of condemnation. And it was not man as first made, but what man became after his sin and punishment, that was thus begotten, as far as concerns the origin of sin and death. (13.3)

19. Augustine's conversion back in Milan in 386 had occurred through his intellectually liberating encounters with Neoplatonic thought, accomplished both through reading groups that gathered around Latin translations of texts of Plotinus and Porphyry and through the sermons of Ambrose, who communicated the legacy of Philo's and Origen's biblical commentaries. Augustine's writings from this period are intriguingly different in tone and in content from his retrospective, theologizing description in the *Confessions*, especially in book 8, site of the famous conversion scene in the garden of Milan; see the discussion in Fredriksen, *Augustine and the Jews*, 123–34 (the years in Milan) and 182–210 (the *Confessions*).

20. Augustine had worked on this issue of gendered fleshly bodies in Eden in his second pass at understanding Genesis "historically," *The Literal Interpretation of Genesis*, written between 401 and 414. On sexual procreation as God's intent for humanity even before the Fall, see *The Literal Interpretation of Genesis* 3.21,33; 9.3,5–11, 19. Had things gone according to plan—without the sin in the garden—sexual procreation would have occurred without (demeaning) pleasure, childbirth without pain (9.10,16–18). For the ways that Augustine's argument fits into the context of the late fourth and early fifth centuries' arguments about virginity, sexual continence, and Christian marriage, see especially Liz Clark, "Augustine and the Early Christian Debate on Marriage"; see also Paula Fredriksen, "Beyond the Body-Soul Dichotomy."

21. For a quick orientation in late ancient theories of human reproduction, see Peter Brown, "Sexuality and Society in the Fifth Century A.D.: Augustine and Julian of Eclanum"; on the ways that this reproductive science helps Augustine to conceptualize both the immaculate conception of Mary

and the benefits of virgin birth for Jesus' sinlessness, see Fredriksen, "Beyond the Body-Soul Dichotomy."

22. Fortunatus quoted this Pauline text, Romans 7.23–25, as well as many others, in his debate with Augustine (*Against Fortunatus* 21). For review of debate and the ways that Fortunatus has the stronger case by appeal to Paul, see Fredriksen, *Augustine and the Jews*, 142–54.

23. In some of the later texts eventually collected in the New Testament canon, these ideas transmute in different ways. The Epistle to the Hebrews works as an extended metaphorizing of Jesus as high priest and as perfect atoning sacrifice, but it does so to argue against the older order of the Levitical priesthood. Revelation, by comparison, maintains a vivid concern with Jewish purity regulations; see David Frankfurter, "Jews or Not? Reconstructing the 'Other' in Revelation 2:9 and 3:9."

24. *Flesh* stood in as a trope for "Jewish" in Christian traditions both orthodox and heretical: Faustus, Augustine's formidable Manichaean counterpart, availed himself of this *contra Iudaeos* heritage in both modalities to criticize catholic tradition as "fleshy" and, thus, "Jewish." In defending his church against this charge, Augustine ended up asserting "true" Christianity's Jewishness, and thus the "flesh" as the true medium of redemption—hence his emphasis on creation, incarnation, and resurrection, which become, against all odds, a defense of Jews and of Judaism as well; see Fredriksen, *Augustine and the Jews*, 213–34 (on Faustus), 235–59 (on Augustine's defense of the flesh), and 260–352 (on Augustine's defense of Jews and Judaism).

Epilogue

1. His concentration on fellow Jews as the audience for his message does not necessarily mean that Jesus had no opinions on or interests in the redemption of the rest of humanity: the broad stream of Jewish apocalyptic tradition in which he stood certainly articulated such. But whatever Jesus' own thoughts on the subject might have been, they left small trace in the gospels' traditions. Both Matthew and Luke begin the mission to the gentiles *after* Jesus' lifetime (Mt 28.19–20, spoken by the risen Christ; Acts 1.8—maybe—and 1.20). This seems to accord with the information that we glean from Paul's letters: if the historical Jesus had left any teachings about how gentiles were to be integrated into the gospel communities, his apostles seem not to have known them, or the confusions and arguments caused by that mission would not have arisen as sharply as they did. Nonetheless, the redemption of "the nations"

who turn to God from idols is a strong theme in the Jewish apocalyptic traditions within which Jesus stood, and the earliest postresurrection movement clearly saw the inclusion of gentiles as a natural extension of itself.

2. Orthodoxy's successful destruction of Marcion's writings means that we have very little to draw on regarding his teachings. He cannot figure equally, then, in this final comparison: we have too little data to frame a secure reconstruction.

3. Some of God's "most hidden" judgments appear in *Against Faustus* 12.44, 13.11; *To Simplicianus* 1.2, 18 (on Jacob and Esau); and *City of God* 15.6 (on the choice of Abel over Cain).

4. Possidius, *Life of Saint Augustine*, 31.1–3; for the historical mis-en-scène, see Peter Brown, *Augustine of Hippo*, chap. 36.

5. The U.S. government, clandestinely selling arms to Ayatollah Khomeini's Iran, diverted some of that money to Nicaraguan contras. When the story came to light, President Ronald Reagan famously "took responsibility" by saying, "Mistakes were made." He then reused the phrase several months later in his State of the Union Address, January 27, 1987; see http://www.miami herald.com/1986/12/07/457328/reagan-mistakes-were-made.

6. See my earlier laments in "What You See Is What You Get" and "Did Jesus Oppose the Purity Laws?"

7. On God's continuing presence in Western culture, Friedrich Nietzsche notwithstanding, Jack Miles, *God: A Biography*, 5, observes:

> No character . . . on stage, page or screen has ever had the reception that God has had. God is more than a household word in the West: he is, welcome or not, a virtual member of the Western family. . . . Playwright Neil Simon published a comedy, *God's Favorite*, some years ago, based on the biblical Book of Job. Few who saw the play had read the biblical book, but there was no need: They already knew what God was like well enough to get the jokes.

Glossary

All Greek, Hebrew, or Latin terms used in the text are translated *in situ* there. What follows is a glossary of some particularly important terms.

Aeon (Gk. *aiōn*; pl. *aiones*): A very long time, an age or epoch; eternity. As a spatial concept, it can mean "the world." In Hermetic texts and cosmogonic Christian ones, the word can indicate various divine beings.

Angelos (pl. *angeloi*): Greek for "messenger" or "envoy," the word is used in the Septuagint to mean "angel." In later Greek thought, pagan or Christian, the word can also indicate lesser deities (thus, Jesus as compared with God the Father in Justin, or Apollo as compared with the highest god in the Oenoanda inscription).

Apocalyptic eschatology: *Apocalypse* in Greek means "revelation," and *eschatology* means "knowledge about final (or ultimate) things." The combined phrase figures in academic discourse to indicate a mood or tradition within Judaism and Christianity, particularly marking the period between 200 BCE and 200 CE, that looked forward to the imminent redemption of the world, often associated with the idea of a resurrection of the dead, the punishment of the "wicked" (variously defined), and the reward of the just.

Cosmos: the Greek word for "order," it comes to indicate "world," especially the organized visible universe. In Ptolemy's model, assumed by our ancient writers, the earth stood at the center of the universe, circled in ascending ranks by the moon, the five planets known to antiquity, and the sun. Beyond the planets lay the realm of the fixed stars. The whole system was usually considered to be ensouled and intelligent, with degrees of perfection (both mental and physical) increasing as one ascended the spheres. Philosophers considered the cosmos divine; other ancient thinkers, such as Paul, held that these divinities, the planetary spheres and astral personalities—*dunameis* ("powers"), *archontes* ("rulers"), *exousiai* ("authorities," 1 Cor 15.24), *stoicheia* ("elements of the universe," Gal 4.9)—were actively hostile to God and would be overcome by Christ at his second coming.

Daimōn (pl. *daimones*): a divinity, often a lesser or local one. Pagan demons might be either good or wicked; Christian ones are almost invariably wicked. The word becomes associated with the idea of lesser gods, therefore gods who are ethnically specific and who have an appetite for blood sacrifices. For this reason, Faustus the Manichee opined that the god of the Jews was clearly a demon (*Against Faustus* 18.2).

Demiurge (Gk. "craftsman"): a term used in Plato and in later Greek texts to identify the divinity, lower than the highest god, who shapes and organizes the visible world.

Diaspora (Gk.; Lat. "dispersion"; Heb. *Galut*, "exile"). In Jewish idiom, any place where Jews live outside of the land of Israel.

Docetism (Gk. *dokein*, "to appear"): A term used to designated the idea in early Christian thought that Jesus only appeared to have flesh, but that his body was actually of a different substance. Heresiologists particularly associated this idea with Gnostic, Valentinian, and Marcionite Christologies.

Ekklēsia: a gathering or assembly of people, perhaps (but not always) for religious purposes. Paul uses the term to mean "the assembly" or "congregation" of baptized Christ-followers; perhaps such functioned as subgroups within the larger synagogue community. In later Christian usage, the term comes to mean "church" (Fr. *église*).

Ethnos (pl. *ethnē*): "Nations" or "peoples"; used in the Septuagint to indicate non-Israelites—hence, pagans. English customarily uses two different words, *gentile* and *pagan*, to translate this single Greek word. In English, *gentile* refers to a person's ethnicity (the person in question is not a Jew), whereas *pagan* refers to a person's religion (the person in question is neither a Jew nor a Christian). The word *pagan*, however, in this sense, is a fourth-century (and derogatory) Christian coinage. In Paul's lifetime, barring conversion, pagans were gentiles and gentiles were pagans: ethnicity and religion stood on the same continuum.

Gnosticism (Gk. *gnosis*, "knowledge"): a term, now much contested, used to indicate those types of religions (whether Christian or not) that posited a relationship of active hostility between the lower, material universe and the upper, spiritual world that was the true home of the believer. This lower realm was arranged and controlled by a wicked and ignorant lower god, Ialdabaoth, often presented in a distorted image of the god of Genesis. Salvation—the liberation of the believer from his entrapment in the material universe—required the acquisition of esoteric knowledge (gnosis). Earlier scholarship had classified both Valentinus and Marcion as types of gnostics. This identification has now been challenged, as has the utility of the broader term itself. The adjective *gnostic* (Gk. *gnostikos*) simply means "knowing."

Hyle (Gk. *hulē*): Aristotle uses this term simply to indicate matter. For later Platonic philosophers such as Sallustius, it was an abstraction, preexistent "formless matter," seen as the material substratum of the visible universe. As the metaphysical opposite of the highest god or of the organizing principle of mind (Gk. *nous*), hyle was totally devoid of characteristics, virtually the definition of nonbeing. Its intrinsic instability was often used to account for various problems with physical body in the material world.

Nag Hammadi Library: A treasure trove of fourth-century Coptic translations of earlier Greek religious texts—gospels, esoteric commentaries on biblical texts, revelations—discovered in Egypt in 1945.

Pleroma: "All" or "fullness." In cosmogonic literature, the term describes zones of a spiritual heaven, often divided between an upper Pleroma (one "closer" to the high god) and a lower Pleroma; both are inhabited by aeons. These aeons proceed from each other in series as linked pairs of divine aspects (gendered male and female, hence a *syzygy*). They are personified in this literature, and emanate ultimately from the high god.

Pneuma: "Spirit" or "breath." In Stoic thought, pneuma is very fine stuff, but it is stuff; in Platonic thought, it is immaterial. Paul uses the term in the Stoic sense; later theology, heavily influenced by Platonic metaphysics, usually presupposes immaterial spirit.

Psuchē: "Soul." A middle term between spirit and flesh, something that animates flesh.

Sarx: "Flesh." The material substratum of the earthly body.

Septuagint: The Greek translation of the Jewish scriptures, done by Greek-speaking Jews in Alexandria, probably completed by the second century BCE.

Soma: "Body." It can be composed of different types of stuff, whether fleshly or spiritual.

Sophia: "Wisdom." In the Septuagint, the word is used particularly for divine wisdom. In Christian cosmogonic texts, Sophia is the youngest, female aeon who wanders from her proper place in the Pleroma in search of the high god (the "One" or the "Father of the All"), thereby inadvertently causing the lower material realm to come into existence.

Zodiac: Twelve constellations, often associated with divinities or cosmic spirits, that in traditional geocentric universes were thought to encompass the circuits of the planets. Antiquity's zodiac thus described the architecture of the visible heavens, mapping an astral reality that was presumed to have immediate effects on life in the sublunar realm. Depictions of the zodiac are found in pagan, Jewish, and Christian sacred spaces.

Works Cited

Ancient Works in Translation

I usually cite biblical texts according to the Revised Standard Version, and intertestamental texts from the *Oxford Annotated Revised Standard Version with Apocrypha*. A larger collection of intertestamental Jewish writings may be found in *The Old Testament Apocrypha and Pseudepigrapha*, 2 vols., edited by J. H. Charlesworth (New York: Doubleday, 1985). An English translation of the Septuagint is readily available thanks to Zondervan Publishing (Grand Rapids, MI, 1970). Where I thought necessary, I adjusted the translations.

Ancient Christian texts in late nineteenth-century translation are readily available online through the Christian Classics Ethereal Library at http://www.ccel.org/fathers. A full list of Augustine's works together with more recent translations may be found in the one-volume encyclopedia edited by Allan Fitzgerald, *Augustine through the Ages* (Grand Rapids, MI: Eerdmans, 1999). Interested readers might also consult the website for the saint himself, maintained by James J. O'Donnell of Georgetown University: http://www.georgetown.edu/faculty/jod/augustine. Collections of Latin texts and English translations are linked to that page. I give below the locations of the translations used in this book, though not infrequently I have adjusted those from the Latin or Greek.

Augustine. *Reply to Faustus the Manichæn*. Translated by Rev. Richard Sto-
     thert. In *Nicene and Post-Nicene Fathers*, ser. 1, vol. 4, 155–345. Grand
     Rapids, MI: Eerdmans, 1974. Originally published 1872.

185

———. *Acts or Disputation against Fortunatus the Manichœn.* Translated by A. H. Newman. In *Nicene and Post-Nicene Fathers*, series 1, vol. 4, 113–24. Grand Rapids, MI: Eerdmans, 1972. Originally published 1872.

———. *City of God.* Translated by Henry Bettenson. Penguin Classics. New York: Penguin, 1972.

———. *Confessions.* Translated by Henry Chadwick. Oxford World's Classics. New York: Oxford University Press, 1991.

———. *Two Books on Genesis against the Manichees.* Translated by Roland J. Teske. In *Two Books on Genesis against the Manichees and on the Literal Interpretation of Genesis: An Unfinished Book.* Fathers of the Church 84. Washington DC: Catholic University Press of America, 1991.

———. *The Literal Meaning of Genesis.* Translated by John Hammond Taylor. 2 vols. Ancient Christian Writers 41–42. New York: Newman, 1982.

———. *Eighty-three Different Questions.* Translated by David L. Mosher. Fathers of the Church 70. Washington, DC: Catholic University of America Press, 1982.

———. *Reply to Simplicianus* Translated by J.H.S. Burleigh. In *Augustine: Earlier Writings*, 376–406. Philadelphia: Westminster Press, 1953.

———. *Unfinished Literal Interpretation of Genesis.* Translated by Roland J. Teske. Fathers of the Church 84. Washington, DC: Catholic University of America Press, 1991.

Clement of Alexandria. *Excerpts from Theodotos*, from the *Miscellanies.* Translated by Werner Foerster. In *Gnosis: A Selection of Gnostic Texts*, vol. 1: *Patristic Evidence*, 146–54, 222–34. Oxford: Clarendon Press, 1972.

Epiphanius. *Panarion.* Translated by Werner Foerster. In *Gnosis: A Selection of Gnostic Texts*, vol. 1: *Patristic Evidence*, 234–38. Oxford: Clarendon Press, 1972.

Eusebius. *A History of the Church.* Translated by G. A. Williamson. Penguin Classics. London: Penguin, 1989.

Irenaeus. *Selections from Against Heresies.* Translated by Werner Foerster. In *Gnosis: A Selection of Gnostic Texts*, vol. 1: *Patristic Evidence*, 127–54. Oxford: Clarendon Press, 1972.

Josephus. *Antiquities of the Jews.* Translated by H. St. J. Thackeray. Loeb Classical Library, 7 vols. Cambridge, MA: Harvard University Press, 1930–1965.

Justin Martyr. *The First Apology According to Justin.* Translated by Alexander Roberts and James Donaldson. In *The Ante-Nicene Fathers*, vol. 1, 163–87. Peabody, MA: Hendrickson, 1994. Originally published 1885.

———. *The Second Apology According to Justin.* Translated by Alexander

Roberts and James Donaldson. In *The Ante-Nicene Fathers*, vol. 1, 188–93. Peabody, MA: Hendrickson, 1994. Originally published 1885.

———. *Dialogue with Trypho*. Translated by Alexander Roberts and James Donaldson. In *The Ante-Nicene Fathers*, vol. 1, 194–270. Peabody, MA: Hendrickson, 1994. Originally published 1885.

Minucius Felix. *Octavius*. Translated by Gerald H. Rendall. In *Tertullian: Apology/De Spectaculis and Minucius Felix: Octavius*, 315–37. Loeb Classical Library. Cambridge, MA: Harvard University Press, 1984.

Origen. *Contra Celsum*. Translated by Henry Chadwick. Cambridge: Cambridge University Press, 1953.

———. *On First Principles*. Translated by G. W. Butterworth. Gloucester, MA: Peter Smith, 1973.

Philo of Alexandria. *Works*. Loeb Classical Library, 10 vols., 2 suppl. vols. Cambridge, MA: Harvard University Press, 1929–1936.

Ptolemy. *Letter to Flora*. Translated by Werner Foerster. In *Gnosis: A Selection of Gnostic Texts*, vol. 1: *Patristic Evidence*, 154–61. Oxford: Clarendon Press, 1972.

Sallustius. *On the Gods and the World*. Translated by Gilbert Murray. In *The Five Stages of Greek Religion*, 211–24. London: C. A. Watts, 1935.

Tertullian. *Adversus Marcionem*. Translated by Ernest Evans. 2 vols. Oxford: Clarendon Press, 1972.

———. *Apology*. Translated by T. R. Glover. In *Tertullian: Apology/De Spectaculis and Minucius Felix: Octavius*, 230–300. Loeb Classical Library. Cambridge, MA: Harvard University Press, 1984.

———. *On the Flesh of Christ*. Translated by Peter Holmes. In *The Ante-Nicene Fathers*, vol. 3, 521–44. Peabody, MA: Hendrickson, 1994. Originally published 1885.

Valentinus, *Gospel of Truth*. Translated by Werner Foerster. In *Gnosis: A Selection of Gnostic Texts*, vol. 2: *Coptic and Mandaic Sources* 55–70. Oxford: Clarendon Press, 1974.

Modern Authors

Allison, Dale C., Jr. *Constructing Jesus: Memory, Imagination, History*. London: SPCK, 2010.

Anderson, Gary. *Sin: A History*. New Haven, CT: Yale University Press, 2009.

Athanassiadi, Polymnia, and Michael Frede, eds. *Pagan Monotheism in Late Antiquity*. Oxford: Clarendon Press, 1999.

Brakke, David. *The Gnostics*. Cambridge, MA: Harvard University Press, 2010.

Brown, Peter. *Augustine of Hippo*. Berkeley and Los Angeles: University of California Press, 1967.

————. "Sexuality and Society in the Fifth Century A.D.: Augustine and Julian of Eclanum." In *Tria Corda. Scritti in onore di Arnaldo Momigliano*, ed. Emilio Gabba, 49–70. Como, Italy: New Press, 1983.

Chadwick, Henry. *Early Christian Thought and the Classical Tradition*. Oxford: Oxford University Press, 1966.

————. *The Early Church*. Harmondsworth, England: Penguin, 1967.

Chaniotis, Angelos. "The Jews of Aphrodisias: New Evidence and Old Problems," *Scripta Classica Israelica* 21 (2002): 209–42.

Clark, Elizabeth A. "Augustine and the Early Christian Debate on Marriage." *Recherches augustiniennes* 21 (1986): 139–62.

————. *The Origenist Controversy*. Princeton, NJ: Princeton University Press, 1992.

DesJardins, Michel R. *Sin in Valentinianism*. Atlanta: Scholars Press, 1990.

Donaldson, Terrence L. *Judaism and the Gentiles: Jewish Patterns of Universalism (to 135 CE)*. Waco, TX: Baylor University Press, 2007.

Dunn, James D. G. *The Theology of the Apostle Paul*. Grand Rapids, MI: Eerdmans, 1998.

Engberg-Petersen, Troels. *Cosmology and Self in the Apostle Paul*. Oxford: Oxford University Press, 2010.

Fitzgerald, Allan, ed. *Augustine through the Ages: An Encyclopedia*. Grand Rapids, MI: Eerdmans, 1999.

Foerster, Werner, *Gnosis: A Selection of Gnostic Texts*. Vol. 1: *Patristic Evidence*. Oxford: Clarendon Press 1972.

————. *Gnosis: A Selection of Gnostic Texts*. Vol. 2: *Coptic and Mandean Sources*. Oxford: Clarendon Press, 1974.

Frankfurter, David. "Jews or Not? Reconstructing the 'Other' in Revelation 2:9 and 3:9." *Harvard Theological Review* 94, no. 4 (2001): 403–25.

————."Where the Spirits Dwell: Possession, Christianization, and Saints' Shrines in Late Antiquity." *Harvard Theological Review* 103, no. 1 (2010): 27–46.

Fredriksen, Paula. *Augustine and the Jews: A Christian Defense of Jews and Judaism*. New Haven, CT: Yale University Press, 2010.

————. "Beyond the Body-Soul Dichotomy: Augustine on Paul against the Manichees and Pelagians." *Recherches augustiniennes* 23 (1988): 87–114.

————. "Did Jesus Oppose the Purity Laws?" *Bible Review* 11, no. 3 (1995): 18–25, 42–47.

————. *From Jesus to Christ: The Origins of the New Testament Images of Jesus.* 2nd ed. New Haven, CT: Yale University Press, 2000.

————. "Hysteria and the Gnostic Myths of Creation." *Vigiliae Christianiae* 33 (1979): 287–90.

————. *Jesus of Nazareth, King of the Jews.* New York: Vintage, 2000.

————. "Judaism, the Circumcision of Gentiles, and Apocalyptic Hope: Another Look at Galatians 1 and 2." *Journal of Theological Studies* 42 (1991): 532–64.

————. "Judaizing the Nations: The Ritual Demands of Paul's Gospel." *New Testament Studies* 56 (2010): 232–52.

————. "Mandatory Retirement: Ideas in the Study of Christian Origins Whose Time to Go Has Come." *Studies in Religion/Sciences Religieuses* 35 (2006): 231–46.

————. "Markan Chronology, the Scene at the Temple, and the Death of Jesus." In *New Views of First-Century Jewish and Christian Self-Definition: Essays in Honor of E. P. Sanders,* edited by Mark Chancey, Susannah Heschel, and Fabian E. Udoh, 246–82. Notre Dame, IN: University of Notre Dame Press, 2008.

————. "Paul and Augustine: Conversion Narratives, Orthodox Traditions, and the Retrospective Self." *Journal of Theological Studies* 37 (1986): 3–34.

————. "What You See Is What You Get: Context and Content in Current Research on the Historical Jesus." *Theology Today* 52, no. 1 (1995): 75–97.

Goodman, Martin. *Mission or Conversion? Proselytizing in the Religious History of the Roman Empire.* New York: Oxford University Press, 1994.

Harnack, Adolf von. *Marcion: The Gospel of the Alien God.* Eugene, OR: Wipf and Stock, 2007. Originally published 1924.

Hirschman, Marc. *A Rivalry of Genius: Jewish and Christian Biblical Interpretation.* Albany, NY: State University of New York Press, 1996.

Hodge, Caroline Johnson. *If Sons, Then Heirs: A Study of Kinship and Ethnicity in the Letters of Paul.* New York: Columbia University Press, 2005.

Isaac, Benjamin. *The Invention of Racism in Classical Antiquity.* Princeton, NJ: Princeton University Press, 2004.

Jonas, Hans. *The Gnostic Religion.* Boston: Beacon Press, 1958.

Klawans, Jonathan. *Impurity and Sin in Ancient Judaism.* New York: Oxford University Press, 2000.

————. *Purity, Sacrifice, and the Temple.* New York: Oxford University Press, 2006.

Knust, Jennifer. *Abandoned to Lust: Sexual Slander and Ancient Christianity.* New York: Columbia University Press, 2006.

King, Karen. *What is Gnosticism?* Cambridge, MA: Harvard University Press, 2003.

Lane Fox, Robin. *Pagans and Christians.* New York: Knopf, 1987.

Layton, Bentley. *The Gnostic Scriptures: A New Translation with Annotations and Introduction.* Garden City, NY: Doubleday, 1987.

Levine, Lee I. *The Ancient Synagogue: The First Thousand Years.* New Haven, CT: Yale University Press, 2000.

Lieu, Judith. "'As Much My Apostle as Christ Is Mine': The Dispute over Paul between Tertullian and Marcion." *Early Christianity* 1 (2010): 41–59.

————. *Image and Reality: The Jews in the World of the Christians in the Second Century.* Edinburgh: T & T Clark, 1996.

Marshall, John. "Misunderstanding the New Paul: Marcion's Transformation of the *Sonderzeit* Paul." *Journal of Early Christian Studies* 20.1 (2012): 1–29.

Martin, Dale B. *The Corinthian Body.* New Haven, CT: Yale University Press, 1995.

Meier, John P. *A Marginal Jew.* 4 vols. New York: Doubleday, 1991–2009.

Miles, Jack. *GOD: A Biography.* New York: Vintage, 1996.

Milgrom, Jacob. *Leviticus 1–16.* New York: Doubleday, 1991.

Mitchell, Margaret M. "Patristic Rhetoric on Allegory: Origen and Eustathius Put 1 Samuel 28 on Trial." *Journal of Religion* 85 (2005): 414–45.

Mitchell, Stephen. "The Cult of Theos Hypsistos between Pagans, Jews, and Christians." In *Pagan Monotheism in Late Antiquity*, ed. Polymnia Athanassiadi and Michael Wrede, 81–148. Oxford: Clarendon Press, 1999.

Mitchell, Stephen, and Peter van Nufflen, eds. *One God: Pagan Monotheism in the Roman Empire.* Cambridge: Cambridge University Press, 2010.

Moll, Sebastian. *The Arch-Heretic Marcion.* Wissenschaftliche Untersuchungen zum Neuen Testament 250. Tübingen, Germany: Mohr Siebeck, 2010.

O'Donnell, James J. *Augustine: A New Biography.* New York: HarperCollins, 2005.

Pétrement, Simone. *A Separate God: The Origins and Teachings of Gnosticism.* San Francisco: HarperSanFrancisco, 1990.

Quasten, Johannes. *Patrology.* 4 vols. Allen, TX: Christian Classics, 1995. Originally published 1950–1978.

Ramelli, Ilaria. "The Philosophical Stance of Allegory in Stoicism and Its Reception in Platonism, Pagan and Christian: Origen in Dialogue with the Stoics and Plato," *International Journal of the Classical Tradition* 18 (2011): 335–71.

Reed, Annette Yoshiko. "The Trickery of the Fallen Angels and the Demonic Mimesis of the Divine," *Journal of Early Christian Studies* 12 (2004): 141–71.

Robinson, James M., ed. *The Nag Hammadi Library*. San Francisco: Harper and Row, 1977.

Rudolph, Kurt. *Gnosis: The Nature and History of Gnosticism*. San Francisco: HarperSanFrancisco, 1987.

Sanders, E. P. *The Historical Figure of Jesus*. London: Penguin, 1993.

———. *Jesus and Judaism*. Philadelphia: Fortress, 1985.

———. *Judaism: Practice and Belief, 63 B.C.E.—66 C.E.* Philadelphia: Trinity Press International, 1992.

Scott, Alan. *Origen and the Life of the Stars*. Oxford: Clarendon Press 1991.

Segal, Alan. *Paul the Convert: The Apostolate and Apostasy of Saul the Pharisee*. New Haven, CT: Yale University Press, 1990.

———. *Two Powers in Heaven*. Leiden, Netherlands: Brill, 1977.

Staples, Jason. "What Do the Gentiles Have to Do with 'All Israel'?" *Journal of Biblical Literature* 130, no. 2 (2011): 371–90.

Stendahl, Krister. *Final Account: Paul's Letter to the Romans*. Minneapolis: Fortress, 1995.

———. "Paul and the Introspective Conscience of the West." *Harvard Theological Review* 56 (1963): 199–215.

Stowers, Stanley. *A Rereading of Romans: Justice, Jews, and Gentiles*. New Haven, CT: Yale University Press, 1994.

Taylor, Joan. *The Immerser: John the Baptist within Second Temple Judaism*. Grand Rapids, MI: Eerdmans, 1997.

Index Locorum

General Index

Adam: allegorical tradition and, 114–15; as antitype of Christ, 32, 34–35; Augustine and figure of, 114–16, 122–25, 176n16, 176n17; free will and, 116, 121–22, 125, 133, 143; original sin and, 115–16, 122–25, 143, 146; Paul and link between sin and, 32–35

Against Faustus (Augustine), 176n13

Against Fortunatus (Augustine), 176n16

Against Marcion (Tertullian), 168n9

angels: fallen, 81–82, 101, 126, 171n25; free will of, 126, 171n23; in Greek pantheon, 166n3; in Hellenistic Judaism, 166n3; as lower gods or messengers (*angeloi*), 54, 166n3

apocalyptic eschatology, 4; delayed or future "end times" and, 61, 90 (*see also* millenarianism and *under this heading*); Gnosticism and, 64; imminent "end times" and, 6–7, 14, 19, 47–48, 90, 93–95, 167n7; Jesus of Nazareth and, 6, 14, 17, 93–95, 135–37, 148, 178n1; Jewish tradition and, 13–15, 19, 48, 50, 96, 137; Justin Martyr and, 90; millenarianism and, 89, 128, 132–33, 146, 173n29;

Paul and, 4, 48–49, 50–52, 60–61, 162n22; and purification or atonement, 6–7, 15–17, 93–95, 158n9; in Q material, 17, 156n3; restoration theology and, 13–14, 94–95; resurrection and, 13, 29–30, 89, 95, 128–29; and second messianic appearance, 48, 167n7; themes of restoration and redemption in, 13–14. *See also* Kingdom of God

asceticism, 17, 112; ascetics as libertines, 73–74; Gnosticism and, 63, 168n11

atonement, 7, 15, 18–22, 93, 97, 131–32, 155–56n2; and redemption, 40–41, 93–95

Augustine of Hippo, 3, 94; Adam as figure and, 114–16, 121–22, 176n16, 176n17; and *ad litteram* (historical) reading, 130–32, 142, 176n16, 177n20; biographical information, 98, 112–13, 146–48, 176n13, 176n14, 177n19; on blood sacrifice, 130–32; conversion of, 177n19; defense of the Jews or Judaism, 178n24; divine justice and mercy as constructed by, 99–100, 124–27, 126–27, 134, 176n16, 179n3;